A Southern Lady's Tea Journey

Andrea "Andy" McDougal

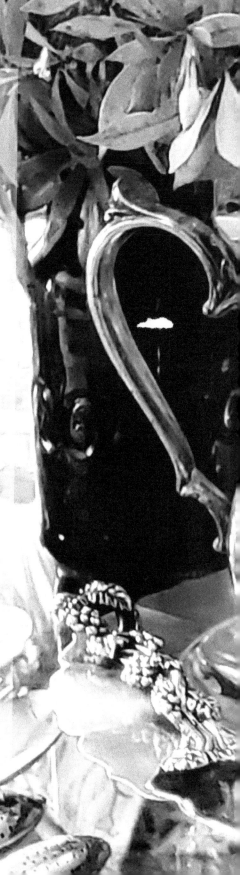

A Southern Lady's Tea Journey

Copyright © 2021 by Andrea L. McDougal

ALL RIGHTS RESERVED

Original photos by Andrea McDougal

Published by:

Tea Garden Publications
18896 Greenwell Springs Road
Greenwell Springs, LA 70739
www.thepublishedword.com

ISBN 978-1-950398-40-9

Printed on demand in the U.S., the U.K., and Australia
For Worldwide Distribution

Dedication

I dedicate this book to my mother, Theadora Ruth Irwin, more commonly known as "Teddie." The name "Teddie" means "Gift of God," and that she has been. Mother has been and continues to be an inspiration in my life. She truly inspired me to write this book, and it has been a journey in which, all along the way, she encouraged me, enlightened me and continuously motivated me to continue to the end.

You will see the chapter, "My Mother, the Key," and that she was. She shared with me the sweetest of memories of things I had not known about her life. They were "such tiny, perfect revelations" they delighted me and gave me great joy!

I hope that, through her encouragement that helped to propel me to finish this book of short stories of my tea-drinking ancestors, my childhood, the places we lived and the tea adventures we had, you will find this book to be colorful, charming and endearing.

At the publication of this book, Mother will be 92 and oh, what a lady she is!

Acknowledgments

I want to thank my husband, Harold McDougal, for the long and intensive hours he put into formatting this book. It was not an easy task. I wrote everything, took all the photos and knew what I wanted it to look like. Then we had to put it all into a book format, which was a little daunting at times! It took many long and grueling hours. I am so thankful for technology! But, as you can see, we have a finished product that I can be so proud to share with you and put my name on! Thank you!

He was a conventional book publisher for close to thirty years, and then in 2004 started a different type of publishing company, where everything is done digitally. This has made it so much more cost effective and faster for many to get their books into print! He has been responsible for putting into print about a thousand books, some by the greatest people in ministry and some by the least—the yet hidden and obscure.

Contents

Legacy
What Is a Personal Legacy?

When a person dies, the mark the individual left on the world represents that individual's legacy.

It is about the richness of the individual's life, including what that person has accomplished and the impact he or she has had on people and places. This is not necessarily richness monetarily, but the richness of the qualities inside of them. Ultimately, the story or details of the quality of a person's life is their legacy that they leave behind, to be passed down to their children and their children's children, their grandchildren and their great-grandchildren.

Introduction

Welcome to my garden. Won't you come on in.
It's fun, you'll see. We'll have some tea and talk of things to be.

Andrea McDougal

A garden is a place of beauty that brings healing, comfort and solace. It is my belief that those who are "lovers of everything tea" are also "lovers of everything beautiful." Our lives are like a beautiful garden; they are what we make of them. I welcome you into my garden, a garden of family, tea, teacups and saucers, teapots, silver and china. I hope you will enjoy it.

I know there are a plethora of tea books that one can purchase that can enlighten you on the knowledge you may be seeking on any subject you are interested in learning about connected to this very tiny word, *tea*. Even though there are only three letters to this subject of tea, it is the biggest and most wonderful three-letter word, because it has a way of introducing, to those of us who have lived a life with tea, a world filled with wonder and beauty. You realize, after many years, that you have been placed on a most remarkable journey—a journey of tea!

We all know that, because of the incredible age of technology we are living in, at the click of a mouse or the touch of a finger, there are unlimited resources of knowledge right before us. Yet, as I write this to you, I realize that the information that has been placed inside a book still remains the richest resource of information you can have at your grasp—whether it is in a physical book that you can turn the paper pages with your fingers, or a digitally produced e-Book that you can download onto your computer, digital reader or smart phone.

Books have been written on the history of tea, how to make the perfect cup of tea, the proper etiquette in drinking tea, ceremonial drinking of tea in Japan or China, the different types of teas and where they are grown and much more. I hope you will find this book to be a little different. I hope you will find it to be a book that is filled with beauty and the love of beautiful things, a delight to your senses—eye candy— but also real-life history. It concerns the pleasures of drinking tea with a friend, a group of friends or a loved one, a husband or precious family member. I also hope that it will stir your heart with thoughts of your tomorrows and renew memories of days that have passed. Those thoughts can once again come to life, and you will be stirred to begin or to extend or enlarge upon your own tea journey.

This book will be historical, on a personal level. I originally had planned it to be a book of seven generations of tea drinkers, going back four generations and forward three generations after me. But I discovered that it goes back many more generations in a city that is known all over the world—New Orleans,

Louisiana, my hometown—and the men and women who helped to make it—my family.

There are several other books that I have written over the years, all Christian, Bible-based books, due to almost fifty years of ministry and travels. To Israel, not knowing that I would receive inspiration and revelation that would change my life and ministry. To many cities in Mexico—Guadalajara, Agua Fria, Juarez, Chihuahua, Zaragoza, Anapra. To Kingston and Ocho Rios in Jamaica. To Lagos in Nigeria, Freetown in Sierra Leone and Accra in Ghana, all in Africa. To Paris, London, Amsterdam and many cities of Scotland. To Sydney in Australia, Auckland in New Zealand, Rome, Aversa and Naples in Italy, many cities throughout the U.S. and others yet to come.

Some might classify these books as self-help or biblically-based books, but I would call them God-help books. Simply put, that is what the Bible does; it teaches us in the way we must walk to have good success!

But now, there is *this* book, and I am very excited about it. Or, should I say, this one and the next two tea books: *A Southern Lady's Tea Adventures* and *A Southern Lady's Teas*. Some might say, "Another tea book to put on a shelf or sit on a table?" To me, it is much more than that; it is the recollection of moments, precious memories with family, friends, mother, children, sisters, husband, loved ones. It is about my family and about our generations of "lovers of everything tea." It is the culmination of tea moments that made up ...

A Southern Lady's Tea Journey.

The Journey Begins

Journey—"The occasion of traveling from one place to another, the process of changing and developing over periods of time!"

am a lover of words! And, on that note, I love knowing what words mean, even the simplest of words. The meanings are like keys that unlock the mystery of what the word is really wanting to convey. I also love knowing the meaning of words because it makes what you are wanting to say or to write much more colorful, and it sheds light on our understanding and gives us much better comprehension. Here our word is *journey*. It means *"the occasion of traveling from one place to another; the process of changing and developing over periods of time!"*

Most of our lives have involved going or *traveling from one place to another*, visiting family, friends, cities, countries, even the cities we live in, meeting new people, experiencing different things. In every step we have taken, every place we have traveled on this journey, we have begun to evolve, *changing and developing over periods of time*. I find this very interesting!

As we begin this tea journey, I will be taking you back in time, to a much simpler time than our current modern-day scenarios. It is my belief that we are probably the same as the generations that have preceded us in many ways, even though many years have passed. I am sure we will all agree that it is technology that has propelled and changed our society and made a considerable difference in the way we live and operate our lives. Yet, we "lovers of everything tea" still have the same hearts, passions and an affinity for everything tea!

As I mentioned in the introduction of this book, it is my desire that your hearts will be stirred to ponder your own journey, whether it began many years ago with the generations that have gone before you or is just now beginning with you and the generations that are ahead.

Many of you reading this book may find that your tea journey of the past or your childhood was much more lavish and elegant, filled with exquisite china, grand tea rooms, beautiful satin and velvet dresses and a much more proper way in which to have tea. For some of you, it may be a journey filled with the simpler things in life, nothing particularly fancy or elegant. All the same, it's a wonderful and glorious journey that has brought you to this day and this book.

It is so interesting to me that with every sip of tea, we did not realize that we were on a journey, taking some of us to places we had never been, sharing tea, information, and friendships with people we had never known before our tea journey. The history of your family or the generations that preceded you may be much different from mine, but hopefully we will find ourselves on mutual ground and walking out our individual tea journeys, either together or separately.

Seven Generations of Tea

Family–
Where life begins & love never ends!

My journey begins before I was born, and I begin my journey with the women in my life who were born before me. I do this because their lives are what influenced my life and helped to create this "tea journey" unawares. Their influences, no matter how great or small, helped to create a passion as a "lover of everything tea" and were used to gently mold me into who I am today. But the greatest hand of influence upon my life was my Creator, He of Heaven and Earth, who created me, fashioned, formed and framed me into what gives Him pleasure!

So, I begin with the women I knew, of course, from the time I was born!

My journey begins in the city of New Orleans, Louisiana. All of our family, both on my mother's side and my daddy's side, lived in New Orleans going back many generations. They were mostly from France and Italy.

Sometime in the early 1900s, at the turn of the century, a young woman boarded a ship from Italy with her family and landed at the Port of New Orleans. Her name was Sarah. She was an Italian girl, ready to begin her life as a young woman, and she was to meet and marry a handsome Frenchman by the last name of Cavelier. She was to be my great-grandmother, and he was to be my great-grandfather.

As many women do when they marry, she took on the traditions of her husband. Even the Bible states that the woman was to learn and cater to the traditions of her husband. The title, *Mother*, in Italian, would have been *Madre*, but she chose to defer to the French tradition and was called by everyone Mère. He, of course, was Père.

I had been with Great-Grandmother, Mère, many times as a child, but once, when I was six, was much different. My memories were heightened because it would be the last time I would get to see her. I remember being dressed as if I was going to church. It must have been in the springtime, because I remember seeing my feet with my white socks and white Sunday shoes, with a little strap that buckled to the side. I was with my mother and my little sister, who was sixteen months younger, and we were both wearing dresses that Mother had made for us.

Mother had always purposed that when we were going somewhere special, she would make sure we were as perfectly dressed as we possibly could be. Everything needed to be ironed in those days. There were no synthetic fabrics. So, we were always dressed without a wrinkle, except for where we sat.

Of course, there were no dryers just yet, and everything that was washed was hung on a clothesline to dry. Many times, when I grew older, in order to get our clothes ready for ironing, I would fill an empty cola bottle with water. It was then set aside and used for sprinkling water on all the clothes that needed to be ironed. I would insert a sprinkler top that had a cork on its end into the cola bottle opening and sprinkle all the clothes that needed to be dampened with water. Then I neatly rolled up each piece of clothing, and it was put aside until it was ready to be ironed.

When our hair was short, Mother would wrap sections of it around her finger and pin them with a bobby pin, to hold the hair in place, thus creating curls. When she would take the bobby pins out and brush our hair, nice blonde curls would flip around the base of our necks, leaving my little sister and me with shiny and stylish little-girl hair styles. Even if our hair was long, there would not be a knot to be found in it. We had perfectly long and shiny pigtails that Mother had braided, and they would fall, one to each side of our faces.

Never a scuff could be seen on our best patent-leather shoes, because Mother kept them clean, and our socks were folded down just right. Because she made most of our clothes, we wore whatever was new in the pattern catalogs. We were not rich by any means, but Mother purposed that her girls would always look proper and carry themselves as well as could be expected.

So, here we were on our way to see our Mère, walking up a cobblestone-like driveway with large areas of very green and perfectly cut grass. There were different buildings within a large complex, with more of the buildings to the right and to the left. But we were walking toward the very large building in the center of everything. It had a portico and a multitude of large, curved arches. As we walked through the opening of one of the archways, the walkway itself was made of brick that seemed to be uneven in places, due to the years of usage. I can remember looking at the bricks, as we were walking under the portico, seeing my shoes as we walked over the worn brick path, and hearing the taps on my shoes as we walked on that brick walkway. It was Mother's practice to put taps on the soles of our shoes, to keep them from wearing out too quickly.

We climbed three flights of wooden stairs that I looked upon intently, and I was relieved when we got to the floor we were going to. Now we were walking on dark, hardwood floors, and once again, I was entranced with the sound of my shoes walking across those wooden floors and was focusing on the appearance of the floors. It was an old building, but well kept. We then entered a large seating area, with floor-to-ceiling windows, as was the tradition of New Orleans buildings and homes.

Mother had lovingly coached us, telling us of Great-Grandmother's condition, which was grave at this point. We were most definitely to be on our good behavior. We were not to misbehave because of Mère's condition, and that of the other people who were there being cared for. It was customary in New Orleans, during those years, that certain orders of nuns would care for the elderly and the sick whose situations were dire. All of the patients there were very ill.

I remember asking Mother if I could speak to Mère, but first I thought, "Should I speak to her?" Mother, of course, responded with a yes and added that we did not want to do anything to overly excite Great-Grandmother. I looked up in that moment, and there was a nun pushing Ma Mère, as Mother called her, in a wheelchair toward us. We went to sit with her by the floor-to-ceiling windows at a long wooden table.

As a little girl of six, I was a bit unraveled, and my heart was sad when I saw the condition of Ma Mère. I pondered what I should say to her and knew that I should say something of comfort. I walked closer to her, with a nervous feeling in my stomach that I know was reflected in my face, touched her on her hand, and told her that I was so sorry that she was ill. She responded to me and assured me that everything would be okay. It was a bit awkward, uncomfortable and sad for me, but I felt compelled, even at that young age, to speak something loving to her. Even as I write this, it is as if I can see the look on my own face that day, as I approached her. I felt her condition so deeply, and I can still feel that almost-sick feeling inside of me and the loss I would soon feel. Shortly after our visit, Ma Mère passed away.

Ma Mère or Great-Grandmother was the matriarch of our family. Now the baton would be passed to her daughters, who would have to pick up and wear their new mantles of authority in their families. This gifted young woman named Sarah who had traveled to the Port of New Orleans all the way from Italy had five daughters and three sons. One of those daughters was my Grandmother, Laurel.

The History of Tea in Italy

Tea had arrived in Italy in the 16th century, to Rome, Venice and Naples, cities of great power, wealth and influence, but tea could only be found in pharmacies for medicinal purposes, healing for the flu. Italy was a country of many generations of staunch coffee drinkers. It was only in 1893 that tea, as a drink, was finally introduced to Italy. Because tea had only been known as a medication until then, it would be a considerable risk for anyone to try to start a business of tea, when this was a country of coffee drinkers.

The very first tearoom was to be opened in Rome by two Colonial British women: Isabel Cargill, daughter of Captain Cargill, Founder of Dunedin in New Zealand, and Ann Maria Babington, a descendant of Anthony Babington, who was hanged in 1586 for conspiring against Queen Elizabeth I of England. These two English women decided that tea needed to be brought to Italy, and thus the first tearoom in Italy was opened in Via Due Macellia. A year after its opening, it was moved to the Piazza di Spagna. You have heard the saying, "All roads lead to Rome." Well, absolutely all the streets of Rome lead to the Piazza di Spagna, to the staircase, to the Bernini Fountain, and then to Babington's Tearoom! It was at the very base of the Piazza di Spagna and was a grand success!

Tea is a daily pleasure, and every cup is a new experience.

–Alfredo Carrai –

Alfredo Carrai is a leader in the new Italian tea revolution
and the owner of La Via del Tè.

23

No matter where you are in the world, you are at home when tea is served.

– Erline Gray –

Whether I am at home or in India or England, to see a teapot and a teacup set before me, I feel no distance, and my weariness is ended!

Andrea McDougal

My Mother, the Key

"A skeleton key is a key that has been stripped of every nonessential part, it has been hollowed out and every serrated edge has been smoothed away, so it can become a master key that will unlock many hidden and obscure treasures."

Andrea McDougal

I happen to love keys, especially old keys and skeleton keys. There is a beauty in them that cannot be found in our modern times or in the making of a modern key. They are made for unlocking and opening things that have been shut and are withholding possible hidden treasures. Did you know that you may have been stripped of every nonessential thing, hollowed out, so to speak, equipping you to unlock mysteries and hidden treasures?

Many times in life, things seem to be obscure or even hidden, as if by lock and key. There are things that, with just a little light shed upon the subject, can bring much understanding into our lives and open up a new world to us that we did not know existed! Even sometimes in the Word of God, things can seem to be hidden from us, and yet we are always given the keys to unlock the mysteries that have been covered over until a specific time, a specific season. When those seemingly-hidden truths are covered over, as we wait for the clarity to come, it is as if an onion skin layer is pulled back, and suddenly, revelation, enlightenment, insight, knowledge, awareness, information will come to us. We are made to have understanding that we did not have before, and things seem to become so very clear to us! There is an old English saying, "All good things come to those who wait." The Scriptures state: *"But those who trust in the Lord will find new strength. They will soar high on wings like eagles. They will run and not grow weary. They will walk and not faint"* (Isaiah 40:31, NLT).

I entitled this part of the book, *My Mother, the Key*. This is due to the fact that just a few simple words that were hidden for so long—kept held in her heart—at the appropriate moment would unlock things that were hidden or obscure. It would be as if a light had begun to shine and illuminate things you had not known of before. It is amazing and oh, so wonderful to have light shed on things that you needed to hear, to see or to understand. So, I am grateful for her words, her wisdom and the things that she so easily unlocked, as a gift, not only to me, but to you too!

I loved hearing her brief stories that she so beautifully articulated. I was astounded and filled with joy when I heard her articulate the simplest words that she would use, and those simple words so solidified and validated her experiences and her own tea journey, almost as if it were happening today in today's tea culture and today's words. This just confirms to me that there is no distance in years. Things have changed, but not really. For me, her simple statements and stories of a bygone time were enchanting and endearing to hear.

Maybe *you* are a key to unlocking the simplest and yet most beautiful things in someone else's life, hidden treasures that need to be brought into the open, to nurture and bless those around you!

The Ritual, or Ceremony, of Tea

When tea becomes a ritual, it takes its place at the heart of our ability to see greatness in small things. Where is beauty to be found? In great things that, like everything else, are doomed to die, or in small things that aspire to nothing, yet know how to set a jewel of infinity in a single moment?

– Muriel Barbery –

I find it wonderful that it is in the small things in our lives that we actually find the greatest of things.

Andrea McDougal

I am sure you have heard the old adage many times, "Some things never change!" Well, the ritual of tea has remained the same. You may call it the ceremony of tea, the habit of drinking tea or the custom of drinking tea. They are all the same. What makes it different is how we make it our own.

What is interesting to me about the habit of drinking tea, the ritual of tea or the ceremony of tea (or however we might choose to call it), is that we never knew we were performing a ritual or acting out a ceremony of tea. We were simply enjoying cups of hot tea with the people we loved the most.

In Japanese culture, when a family or a group of friends sat down to have their ceremony of drinking tea, it symbolized to them purity, tranquility and respect. Their ritual took great preparation. The teapot had to be prepared properly, water was precisely heated, and the correct amount of loose tea would be added to the pot. The teacups were placed on a proper type of table (one that sat close to the floor), and the guests, or those who were to participate in the drinking of the tea, would need a pillow to sit on. Once everything was done, and every amount of care was given to the drinking of tea, it was all considered to be part of the ceremony of tea!

Every step you take, no matter how simple or commonplace it may seem to you or someone else, no matter how you dress for your first cup of tea in the morning, where you sit or what kind of vessel you drink from, every step you take is your habit of drinking tea. In other words, it is your personal ritual, your ceremony of tea. There is no set way, but how you choose to perform it.

As I wrote these steps in the Japanese ceremony of tea, I had to smile. In a way, it is exactly how we perform our ceremony, or ritual, of having a daily cup of tea.

The Victorian tea ceremony, the ceremony of drinking tea during the Victorian Age, was interspersed with garden teas and promenades around the estates or, as in our day and time, a walk through the garden. This was a part of their ritual, ceremony or habit of having tea. It was their common practice of tea.

I am sure of one thing that I have seen throughout the years: Whether you drink your tea from a mug in your daily ritual of tea or a beautiful and most elegant teacup, whether you use a tea bag or loose tea, whether you dress for tea, where you sit to have your tea, what time of the day you choose to have tea, or if you call it afternoon tea or high tea, it is your personal ceremony of tea, your own ritual. It is your preferred habit for experiencing tea.

There are few hours in life more agreeable than the hour dedicated to the ceremony known as afternoon tea.

– Henry James –

Your ritual, or ceremony, of tea is simply your common practice of serving or having tea!

Andrea McDougal

Mother Joins the Tea-Drinking Club

"At the age of twelve, I officially became a part of the tea-drinking club. What a delight it was!" –Mother, Teddie Irwin –

It was customary, as my mother was growing up, that every day there was afternoon tea! Every day was a ritual; every day there was the ceremony of experiencing tea. She and the other ladies of our family were not aware that they were experiencing a tea ritual or a ceremony; they were simply having their afternoon tea, either alone or together. Whether it was just with Ma Mère, her mother (and my grandmother), there was still afternoon tea, and as often as possible they would share it together.

Mère's daughters who were not working a job and who lived close by and not in another city would gather for afternoon tea. If it was conducive for everyone, they would gather at Mère's or at one of the homes of the daughters who lived close by. There were many walks to a neighborhood bakery to get delicious dainties to go with their afternoon tea.

At this time in the history of this group of women who loved their ritual of afternoon tea, I had not yet been born. Mother was only a young girl of about twelve herself. Mère had five daughters, and it is interesting to me that I am the oldest of five girls. But during this time, there were only four girls and three sons. That was because her youngest daughter, Hazel, had already passed away.

There was, of course, my grandmother, Laurel, who was in New Orleans and Great-Aunt Catherine, who lived close by. My Great-Aunt Margaret, once she was married, mostly lived in Mobile, Alabama. And there was Great-Aunt Helen, whose home, many years later, I remember, oh, so very vividly, visiting many times and spending time with my cousins, Milton and Shirley. I also remember seeing her garden filled with beautiful and colorful gladiolas. During the time of Mother's growing up, if they went to Catherine's home for tea, she would always serve them something to eat, either a light meal or some pastries (that were oh, so delicious) from one of the neighborhood bakeries.

When it came my time to be a part of this tea-drinking club, I, too, would experience the many walks taken with my grandmother or a great-aunt to one of New Orlean's well-known bakeries for jelly donuts, cream puffs or chocolate éclairs. It has always amazed me that I have yet to this day found any pastries that were quiet as delicious as those to my taste buds—not a jelly donut, not an éclair, nor a cream puff.

Believe me, over the years, whenever I entered a bakery, I would seek out those special items to taste and see if I could find those same flavors once again. I can honestly say that those flavors have not been found to enter my mouth ever again. Nothing has ever come close to what I knew during those years of growing up in this wonderful family.

Let me say here that these Italian/French women were great cooks, but sometimes they were pressed for time, and the neighborhood bakery would always have what they needed to go with a cup of hot tea! Catherine would always serve hot tea for her sisters, her mother, Mére, and any nieces who were attending, but she herself would never drink tea. She was more of a coffee drinker.

It was very customary that coffee was the drink of the morning. Most of the women would drink their morning coffee with chicory, along with the man of the house, their husbands. That was what gave you the quick kick you needed to get you out the door and off to work. It was not for the faint of heart, for this was a very strong coffee that would seem to bite your tongue. But, as the morning would pass and the women of the houses pursued their housecleaning and

cooking, or they were off to their own jobs, they all looked forward to their special time together, to have their afternoon tea.

These women were not clothed in satin or velvet, and no fascinator graced their heads. But the best of each person's china or porcelain would be brought out to dress the table for the women of the family.

Many afternoon teas were shared on Sundays at Great-Aunt Helen's home. I have many fond memories of her perfectly-painted green house dressed in gladiolas that stood tall and erect against it.

It was a delightful Sunday afternoon, and there was much activity as everyone began to arrive. There was seating for eight at Helen's kitchen table. I knew this table well (and her kitchen), for it would be one that I would sit at to eat a bite of King Cake at Mardi Gras time, and I would get the baby hidden in the cake. It would be where I would sit to learn to embroider my first piece of hand stitchery. But those events would take place in years to come.

Mére had arrived early, and then there was Aunt Catherine. She had spent most of her morning preparing something special for the afternoon tea. Grandmother and Mother were there, Mother asking Aunt Helen what she could do to help. Grandmother had brought her famous pineapple upside-down cake, and Aunt Catherine had brought some freshly baked eggplant, done the Italian way, stuffed with fresh New Orleans shrimp.

It was a special Sunday because Aunt Margaret and Uncle Lenny had come to town to visit and stay the weekend with her sisters and mother. Aunt Helen's daughter, Shirley, would also be joining them for afternoon tea.

As the kettle began to whistle, everyone was taking their place at the table. The table had been set, as Mother put everything that was needed for the meal in its proper place.

The meal would be eaten, along with their cups of hot tea.

Before the meal was served, you could hear the ladies begin to add the sugar and milk to their tea. And then there was the sound, the voice of a twelve-year-old girl who spoke quiet boldly. This twelve-year-old, not yet knowing it, was about to begin her own tea journey and go to the next level.

She had set many a table, helped in serving tea to her aunts and grandmother, and had taken many a walk to a neighborhood bakery or grocery store to help get the perfect pastry or other grocery store item and had also helped to clean everything up after many an afternoon tea. The one thing she had *not* done was to have her first cup of tea! This twelve-year-old girl was my mother.

When Mother told me this story, she said that she asked her Aunt Helen if it was all right for her to say something. When she was given permission, her statement went something like this: "How does someone get to join this tea-drinking club?" There was complete silence for what seemed like an eternity to Mother. The clanking of the teaspoons against the teacups as the ladies stirred their hot tea came to a complete stop, and the clamoring of all the voices there became silent.

Then, out of the midst of that total silence, my Grandmother finally spoke, "Is there an extra teacup and a bit of tea for another to join us?" Immediately Great-Aunt Helen pulled out another teacup and saucer, and it became the teacup and saucer my mother would get to use every time she had tea at Aunt Helen's home. It was a lovely Homer Laughlin teacup and saucer. In this way, a new part to my mother's tea journey began, one that would eventually enrich my own tea journey—and hopefully yours as well.

Remember the tea kettle is always up to its neck in hot water, and yet it sings.

You never know how strong a woman is until you put her in hot water.

– Eleanor Roosevelt –

And So, the Journey Continues

My mother spent so many more incredible days of her life with these amazing and wonderful tea drinkers than I did—being born in 1929, the year the stock market crashed and the Great Depression was ushered in. A whole new way of living, or should I say,

surviving, was introduced. Life was not easy. No, it was not easy at all. She told me there were times when she and my grandmother lived with Great-grandmother, "Ma Mère." How fond were her memories of those days!

Père, my great-grandfather, passed away in 1933, so Mother never had any memories of him. But from the time of being a little girl, she spent many hours and days and maybe even weeks with her Mère. Now, she was to live with Mère for a whole year.

Mother's memories go back to her being a young girl, before she joined the tea-drinking club. As she became a little older, she remembers the teatimes that she got to observe and then participate in as an active tea drinker. Even when she was just a little girl and had not yet joined the family tea-drinking club, she had helped to set the tables for afternoon tea, placing a proper lace tablecloth over Mère's mahogany table, placing the pastries on their proper plate, pulling from Mère's cabinet the lovely cups and saucers that were always used just for these special teatimes. She would also help in the kitchen with cooking, cleaning and whatever else needed to be done to make everyone's teatime a pleasant one.

Every day, no matter what was going on, around 3 pm to 6 pm, at some point everyone would take a break, time was set apart, and there would be afternoon tea. Mère would have a daughter or two who could come for afternoon tea, to sit and talk and share in the moments of refreshing, through their conversation sharing their day and drinking a pot of hot tea.

Now, some years have come and gone, Mother had already joined the coveted tea-drinking club, she was now in her senior year of high school, and Mère had taken a job for a wealthy man in New Orleans. He lived in a very lovely three-story home in a much-desired neighborhood on Napoleon Avenue. He was a widower with three children. He had hired Mère as a live-in caregiver and nanny for his small children. She was also to cook and care for the household. During this time, the gentleman of the house was very ill and was in a sanatorium with tuberculosis. The home was quite large and, therefore, overwhelming for Mère to take care of, with the cooking and cleaning and caring for the three children while their father was convalescing. So, Mère invited my Grandmother (who was her daughter) and my Mother and Mother's little brother Terry to move into the house and help her with the duties that were before her. During this time, Mother had already become a part of the family's tea-drinking club, as we saw in the last chapter.

Even now, every afternoon, there was a tradition, a ritual that would take place, no matter what else was going on. Mother remembers it very vividly. Mère would begin to boil the water for their cups of tea. From any floor of the house, Mother could hear the water going into the kettle and the gas stove being turned on. Then, as the fire would heat the kettle, the whistle would begin to let everyone know that tea was about to be observed.

Their tea was always brewed from loose tea, and Mother can remember watching Mère scoop the loose tea into the teapot, to be steeped into a delicious and refreshing drink suitable for those she loved so much. Every afternoon, Ma Mère, Grandmother, Mother and Terry would sit and enjoy their teatime together.

Come, let us have some tea and continue to talk about happy things.

– Chaim Potok –

*But indeed I would
rather have nothing but tea!*

– Jane Austin –

Lovers of Everything Tea & Everything Beautiful

Tea is quiet, and our thirst for tea is never far from our craving for beauty.

– James Norwood Pratt –

This is a definite to me, that those who are "lovers of everything tea" are the purest romantics. They love beautiful china, intricate lace tablecloths, napkins with embroidery or trimmed with Battenburg lace or with crocheted trims and beautiful accoutrements used in the serving of tea, exquisite teapots and the most glorious teacups and saucers. These "lovers of everything tea" are "lovers of everything beautiful," no matter their choice or habit, ritual or ceremony of having a cup of tea!

Have nothing in your house that you do not know to be useful or believe to be beautiful.

–William Morris–

My Time Had Come
"I am born"

As I mentioned previously, my family on Mother's side, as well as on Daddy's side, were many generations steeped in the city of New Orleans. There, we go back many generations, coming from mostly parts of France (around Paris) and Italy.

My grandma that you have not met yet owned a boarding house in New Orleans. Boarding houses were very popular in those days. They provided both housing and meals.

World War II had come to an end, and the soldiers had returned home. My daddy, a Marine who served in World War II, had been in Japan when the flag was raised over Iwo Jima. He was now living at his mother's (my grandma's) boarding house, and Mother, Grandmother and Terry just happened to be living there. This is how my parents met. It was a collision course of love, and they were married at the boarding house on Christmas Eve, with family and friends gathered to celebrate. They would continue living in New Orleans for some time.

In those days, one of the cutting-edge jobs to get into was in the new field of television, much like computers today. Daddy was wanting to have a career in something that would allow him to properly provide for my mother and the children who would come. He had heard of a school in Louisville, Kentucky, and they soon decided to move there. During his time of study, he also had to work to support the family. He would get up every morning around 2 am to do the job of a milkman, making his deliveries between 4 and 6 am. Then he would go to school for eight hours a day.

During my parents' time in Louisville, I was conceived, and this little New Orleans girl would be born on March 10th, 1949 on a very cold and snowy day in Louisville, Kentucky.

We lived on the third floor of an apartment house. To wash our clothes, including my diapers, Mother would have to go down three flights of stairs and back up three flights of stairs. So, during that time, Daddy provided her with a diaper service, which she loved.

Of course, I was the delight of my parents, as every child is. But my parents saw something in me that went beyond the norm. And, from that point on, my father and mother both, in their eyes, saw something of greatness. Mother always told me that I was their rising star and a gift from God. They would have four more daughters, and each would be the apple of their eyes, and each daughter would be loved equally the same and shine bright in Daddy's eyes and in his heart. Being the oldest of these five girls, I could see it in his eyes, the overwhelming love, adoration and desire for greatness in each of his girls. Daddy would always consider me almost to be a child prodigy, even though I was never able to be exactly that.

Almost immediately after graduating from school and having an engineering degree, Daddy was contacted by a company in Bloomington, Indiana. They told him they were sure they were going to hire him because of his record in school, but they wanted to meet him and interview him personally first. He got the job, returned to Louisville to get Mother and me, and we moved to Bloomington. There the second daughter in the family would be born, and I would have a close companion and playmate. Her name was Lillian.

After some time of working in Bloomington, Daddy became desirous of us moving back home to the city he loved and the family he was missing. And so we did.

Before I formed you in the womb, I knew you, and before you were born I consecrated you; I appointed you a prophet to the nations.
— Jeremiah 1:5

Children are the inheritance of the Lord.
— Psalm 127:3

Like arrows in the hands of a warrior are children born in one's youth.
— Psalm 127:4

My First Memory

"As a Child"

I was about two years of age when I can recall my first memory concerning where we lived, what our homes were like and the introduction of family members into my very young life.

My first memory of our home was of a peaceful and serene life. I remember a few things about the house. I know that we lived on South Galvez Street in the heart of the city. This home was what was available when my parents, myself and my baby sister, Lillian, moved back to New Orleans. Another home, just a block away, would soon become available, and my memories would become much more intense as I began to age.

My first memory, after we returned home, was at that first house. I remember sitting in the living room by myself on the arm of a stuffed chair. The arm itself was also stuffed, and I was a very tiny thing, sitting up there. I must have been sitting very close to the open window, because I was intently watching raindrops hitting the window screen, then streaming down and going into every fine opening of that screen. Each of those drops either made its way down to the bottom or was diverted along the way. They were all moving downward, but they all stopped at different spots on their way down. It was amazing to observe.

I remember Mother opening a door from another room and looking in to see what I was doing. She seemed concerned that I was sitting so close to the window during a rainstorm. I turned and looked at her and said, "Mother, do not worry. I am all right." I assured her that I was safe and would be just fine.

It amazes me that at such a young age I could communicate with my mother like that, but I can remember the details of it as if it had just happened yesterday. Daddy and Mother always said I did everything earlier than other children.

I told you this story because it was my very first memory. My second memory would come sometime later. I was about to meet my very first relative. This would be one of my great aunts, a daughter of Ma Mère and Ma Père. She was Great-Aunt Margaret.

Margaret was the one who lived in Mobile, Alabama, with her Greek husband, Uncle Lenny. Uncle Lenny was a successful shoe salesman and a very artistic and sought-after window dresser. For years, he kept Mother in many pairs of expensive shoes that had been used in his window displays.

One day they came to visit. I did not realize that they had come to take my little sister, Lillian, back with them for a visit, all the way to Mobile. When I learned of it, my heart was broken because I was not being invited, and because I would be separated from my tiny sibling and closest friend. I cried very emotional tears, and I can remember Mother telling them to go ahead and leave, that I would be okay. It is strange to me that, like so many of my other memories, I can feel the pain, or should I say, the ache in my heart of being separated from my sister. It was very real.

I don't know how much time passed, if it was a day or days, but I, too, would have a visit in their home, along with my little sister. I don't remember the trip or anything else except the bedroom Lillian and I shared while we were there.

I must say here that these amazing women of our tea-drinking club and family were the most immaculate housekeepers! There was never a spec of dust to be seen anywhere in their homes. Everything was always spotless, and that was the case in Aunt Margaret's home too.

In Mobile, our room had two little twin beds, and we each slept in one of them, with crisp white sheets and a light blanket. I can remember asking my little sister if this was the same bedroom she had slept in when she first stayed there without me. She said no, but she couldn't remember where it was that she had slept. I was just happy to be there with her this time.

Over to the left of where our beds were, I could see a tall, blonde-colored chifforobe (a French word used in the South for a piece of furniture utilized as a closet for hanging clothes). On the very top of this piece of furniture were two little purses covered in a red tartan plaid fabric. Now these little purses had not been there when we went to bed. So, after we had gone to sleep, someone, either Aunt Margaret or Uncle Lenny, had put the sweet little gifts there for us to see when we woke up in the morning. We loved them. I cherished that sweet gift from my aunt and uncle for many years to come.

All of that was leading up to what is next. We were dressed and went into the rest of the house to where our breakfast would be served. We must have arrived a little late

the first night, or we had fallen asleep during the long drive and were carried into our room and dressed for bed. I say this because I have no remembrance of any other part of the house, only that little room where we slept. Aunt Margaret had gotten us out of bed and helped us to dress for the day, and I remember as we walked into another room, Uncle Lenny was there, and he asked if we had slept well and if we liked our tartan purses. I declared, "We love them, thank you!"

We talked some more, but my eyes continued to be distracted by what I was seeing. There was the most lovely table I had seen to this point of my life as a tiny girl (at least that I could recall or knew what I was seeing). I was impressed, if a child of my age could be impressed. Maybe I should say "intrigued." Anyway, it caught my attention. I can't tell you what we ate, but I can remember the beauty and charm of what was on our table.

Even though most of the pieces of china remained in the china cabinet, the few pieces that graced our table were a sheer delight to my eyes. There were teacups gracing my aunt and uncle's plates for breakfast, with little golden teaspoons. On the table was a small bouquet of what I believed to be orange flowers and a lovely teapot. I thought that I should surely need to have it, for I had never seen anything quite as pretty. Of course, there was no tea for us at this early age. That would be for years to come.

I later learned that the beautiful pieces that filled my heart with envy that day were made by Noritake. Noritake was very popular during the 30s, 40s and 50s and remains so up until our current day. This beautiful pattern, called Jasmine, was produced in 1933 in Noritake, Japan and had been a wedding gift handed down to Aunt Margaret and Uncle Lenny from his great-aunt.

Their lovely china cabinet not only contained beautiful pieces of the Noritake Jasmine, but also many other things of beauty. There were beautiful porcelain flowers and other items from their travels together over the years of their young marriage. Of course, I was much too young to appreciate or to understand anything about tea or china or porcelain or Noritake, but what I could see coming into my eyegate was definitely beautiful.

As I pondered this, while writing this part of my story and remembering what I had experienced at that young age, I must say that it brought back to my remembrance a similar situation, when two charming little girls, two of my young granddaughters—Hannah Grace and Sarah Marie—came to visit my home. They were definitely close to the same ages as myself and my little sister during that time. Hanna, the oldest of the two, stood in front of my china cabinet, which was made of white wicker. The two doors, the side panels and the shelves were glass, and gracing the glass shelves were beautiful pieces of blue and white dinner plates, cups and saucers, and tabletop teapots I had purchased on a trip inside the U.S. and also while in London. It also hosted numerous treasures from other countries and gifts that had been given to me. As she stood in front of that treasure-filled cabinet and gazed upon what was before her, she turned to me and said, "Oh, Nonnie, it is so beautiful!" I believe she experienced what I had experienced when I first caught a glimpse of beauty in the world of being "a lover of everything tea." That day the same two precious granddaughters had a tea party with a couple of the prettiest little teapots and cups and saucers in my dining room.

Now, I cannot tell you how long we stayed at Aunt Margaret and Uncle Lenny's home or anything else about our stay, except that Uncle Lenny loved baseball and took me to a baseball game one night. I don't know if these were major league teams or minor league teams. I *do* know that there were a lot of people there, some bright lights, a lot of music and popcorn and hot dogs to eat.

I also know this: throughout the years to come, there would be many cups of tea and special afternoon lunches and chocolate éclairs and cream puffs with Aunt Margaret and Uncle Lenny and the other members of our family's tea club. It would take many years for me to understand our ritual, or ceremony, of tea and the tea journey that we were on. But, as I look back, it was such a great adventure!

"A teapot so beautiful I thought I should have it."

It is always time for tea.

A cup of tea solves everything.

Mother's Teacup

"There is nothing better for breakfast, or any other time of day, than a cup of hot tea and toast!"

– Mother, Teddie Irwin –

There are so many memories that I can share, but I feel that those must be saved for another time and another book. I planned that this book should be dedicated to the highlights of my tea journey.

We were now living on Johnson Street. There were many lessons about food that would come later in another neighborhood. I will say that at this house, we were right next door to a small neighborhood grocery store, and I can remember Mother giving me a dime and telling me to go next door and get a loaf of bread.

I have been flooded with memories from our years at this home. We had a side screened-in porch, and when you walked through the door into the house, there was our kitchen. I remember mostly a wooden table and chairs. This was where Mother lovingly prepared our meals. I so loved being in the kitchen, because we were with her, watching everything she was doing.

My sister Lillian and I would each stand in a chair, leaning over, trying to get close to the food, so we could get a taste. Because Lillian was younger and smaller than I, she would kind of sit on the table, or stand, but we were both always leaning into what Mother was doing, intently watching her every move. I remember her peeling potatoes for supper, making a pudding from scratch and putting a taste of it on her finger and letting us have a taste of what was to come.

Then, always, sometime around 3 pm, it would be time for afternoon tea. I had noticed that Mother would break for her afternoon cup of tea, and she would use the same teacup and saucer every day. The fire would be turned on under the kettle, and out came the box of loose tea. She would open the cabinet door to where one of her prized possessions sat, waiting to be used. Mother would only drink from bone china when she had her afternoon tea. She is now 91 and soon will be 92, and she has always had a special cup from which she would drink her afternoon tea.

It really was a thing of beauty, a bone china teacup and saucer. It was almost translucent when you would hold it up to a light or a ray of sunshine coming through a window. This little beauty was dressed in delicate swags of red roses, with banners of gold, and it was edged in thin, red lines. Oh, what an exquisite work of art this cup and saucer were! They were made during the time of Occupied Japan, and it is very difficult to find such a treasure these days.

Mother recently told me why she wanted to only drink from a bone china teacup, besides the great delight it was just to look at it. She said the teacup rim of fine bone china is very thin, and because of that, when you drink from bone china, the tea would simply glide onto your tongue with pure tea flavor! Bone china teacups will never stain. You never have to bleach them or scrub a stain away, and that is because the inside of the cup is so fine and smooth. It never holds color or the flavors of anything else that has graced it. She also said that the tea simply tasted better.

Tea was inexpensive, so it made a nice drink to offer family and friends when they came to visit, and it made everyone feel specially treated. Not many really understood the benefits of tea or what it was doing to their bodies. All they knew was it was a great way to get a quick pick-me-up in the afternoon, one that would carry them through the early evening hours.

Mother's teacup and saucer that she used for her afternoon tea, that exquisite fine bone china, was the only teacup and saucer she would use for that purpose. Then, there were those days when Mother would have company for afternoon tea, and out would come pretty teacups and saucers of the same beautiful pattern.

Mother did not own a china cabinet. But, at this house in New Orleans, above her kitchen counter were sweet cabinets with glass doors that displayed the beautiful pieces of china she had acquired.

A Kingdom of Tea Drinkers

King Charles the Second of the Stewart Dynasty needed a queen! In 1662, he married Catarina de Braganza of Portugal (Catherine of Braganza). Catherine thus became the Queen of England, Scotland and Ireland.

They were of the aristocracy and Historic Royal Court during the Great Fire of London and the Great Plague. During that time, Queen Catherine stated that she would make Great Britain, "a kingdom of tea drinkers," and that she did.

I frequently dream of having tea with the Queen.

– Hugh Grant –

We live
by faith
not by sight.

2 Corinthians 5:7

Why Tea Makes You Feel Good & Makes Everything Okay

A brew will see you through!

Have you ever noticed that so many tea quotes rave over the marvels of tea? Those who are lovers rave over the benefits of tea and have such a passion for this wonderfully marvelous drink called tea, finding it to be healing, comforting and soothing. It helps us even in our worst times and gives us a sense of wellbeing. Well, it's all true and is based on science, based on how tea is made, and yet it is simple, and it is factual. Tea really does all of these things for us—and even more!

There is no trouble so great or grave that cannot be diminished by a nice cup of tea.

– Bernard Paul Heroux –

I expect I shall feel better after tea.

– P. G. Wodehouse –

Tea has some components in it that do all that is written about it. We know that tea has caffeine, but it also has a natural component, an amino acid called L-theanine. This amino acid is found to have a relaxing effect on the mind and reduces anxiety and stress! L-theanine also sharpens your concentration and boost your memory, and when you combine caffeine with this amino acid, something takes place. Your brain activity is increased, and your mood is improved. When brain activity is increased, and your mood gets a boost, it gives you a sense of relaxation and a sense of wellbeing that only a cup of tea can provide!

Tea is to the body
what music is to the soul.

– Carlene Gray –

Tea, A Familiar Companion

Tea has been my constant companion. It is with me every day. It brings comfort and healing when I need it. When friends call, they are filled with delight and made to feel special, and they leave my home refreshed with a little bit of royalty cloaking them.

Andrea McDougal

There is nothing better for me on a rainy day than to be able to lie down on my wicker chase with beautiful pillows, a comfy quilt, a favorite magazine to read and slowly sip a cup of hot tea.

Andrea McDougal

THANK GOD FOR TEA! WHAT WOULD THE WORLD DO WITHOUT TEA? HOW DID IT EXIST? I AM GLAD THAT I WAS NOT BORN BEFORE TEA!

You are my cup of tea!

The Journey to Meet My Grandmother

I inquired, "What shall I call you?" She responded, "You shall call me Grandmother."

Once again, I found my feet upon a wooden floor, a very long wooden floor. Dressed as nicely and perfectly as a five-year-old little girl could be dressed, in a dress my mother had made, with freshly combed hair, my buckle shoes and socks, and I was holding the hand of either my mother or my dad. I can only remember holding the hand as we walked with one of my parents for my little hand was nestled into a larger hand, with a lengthy arm going up to someone much taller than I.

We were walking through what I learned to be barracks on the air base. It was not until I was visiting with my grandmother some years later, and we drove by the buildings that we had walked through that day, that I was told what they were— barracks.

When we finished walking through the barracks and had not yet hit our destination, we walked through what seemed to be another very long walk on a wooden floor, another barracks, one after another, until we would get to where we were intended to be— the hospital at Keesler Air Force Base in Biloxi, Mississippi.

My grandfather had been stationed at an Air Force Base in England, and that was why they had lived there for many years. He was an instructor in the Air Force and taught the young men stationed there. My grandparents and their son, my Uncle Terry, lived in England for many years.

They were sent home earlier than expected due to my grandmother being very ill. They were transferred to Keesler so that she could get the best care possible. She was given only six months to live. But, to God be the glory, that was in 1954, and she lived until 1982, when I was 32 and was expecting my fourth child, Elizabeth.

I can remember my first conversation with my grandmother. She was not in the hospital. At least I am not aware that she was. I feel that we had been talking, but my first words to her, that I can remember, were to ask, "What should I call you?" She asked me, "What do you call your daddy's mother?" And I replied, "Grandma."

Due to the years of my grandmother living in England, her speech was very prim and proper, with a heavy British accent, and she would pronounce her words very different from the way we would say them, either in the South or the whole of the U.S.

Thank God for tea!
What would the world do without tea?
How did it exist?
I am glad I was not born before tea.

– Rev. Sydney Smith –

In England, everything stops for tea.

My grandmother replied, "You will call me Grandmother." And so it was that I now had a grandmother in my life.

I had known of Grandmother long before we met. She would send us packages of goodies at Christmas and other times, filled with wonderful delicacies to eat that she would make. Some of those treats would be small pecan pies, divinity fudge, stuffed dates with pecans and marshmallow cream, cookies, candied pecans and many other wonderful treats.

One of the first packages I remember Mother getting from Grandmother included, not only her homemade delights, but also beautiful woolen fabrics from Scotland and England. I can remember that package arriving and seeing the beautiful woolen fabrics and their colors. A beautiful green piece of woolen fabric still sticks out in my memory. I took the fabrics out of the box and asked Mother what she was going to do with them. She replied, "I am going to make coats for you and your sister." And that she did!

There would come many visits to Grandmother's home when they were stationed at Keesler. At Christmas, Thanksgiving and other holidays, we would go to visit them at the base, or my grandparents and Uncle Terry would come to our home. My young sister and I would eventually begin to spend part of our summers at their home. When other sisters were born, they would reach an age when they, too, would go for visits at Grandmother's house.

Grandmother's Collections

A collector is a gatherer of beautiful things.

Andrea McDougal

I know what you are waiting to hear about—tea, teacups, teapots and teatime! Grandmother had a wonderful sturdy teapot, a kettle and a beautiful collection of teacups from her time in England. Others were handed down to her from her mother, Mère, and her grandmother.

During my visits with Grandmother, I could not keep my eyes off of her massive collection of Eric Stauffer's Hummel-like creations. When there was nothing to do, I would sit in front of Grandmother's beautiful German-made china cabinet, with wood inlay and curved glass doors. This beautifully ornate cabinet was home to her very large collection of Eric Stauffer's German figurines of boys and girls doing everything imaginable. There was a little girls sitting and holding an umbrella, hens following a little girl, a young boy playing a violin, a little boy and girl leading a flock of geese, and the list goes on.

I was mesmerized as I sat on her perfectly clean floor, with my legs folded in front of me and my hands supporting my chin in a dreamy world, having never experienced such a wonderful place before and seeing a collection that was so enchanting to me of little boys and girls in the cutest of outfits, doing the most wonderful things. This scenario, for me, would take place many times over the years, and every time, as I sat looking intently upon the little girls and boys of Eric Stauffer, I would find my eyes being drawn away, as if something else was demanding my attention. I would look to the right of this very loving collection, and there was another cabinet, not as tall and grand, but still requiring me to look upon it. It was a lovely mid-century piece, and the whole cabinet, except for its frame, was glass and the shelves were glass, and there I would see such lovely teacups and saucers that I became very intrigued. At times, I would glance at what was before my eyes and look away, but then there were times when I felt compelled to look at what was before me.

I can even remember thinking I needed to look more intently at what I was seeing. I needed to give it my full attention and look beyond what was first getting my glance. I was to look deeper, beyond the first layer that was before me. And, as I did, another world of beauty was opened to me.

There were cups and saucers dressed in carnations, some with golden rims and golden handles, one with peaches and peach blossoms, beautiful designs, with roses and other flowers.

Some even took on an oriental look, with an iridized glaze different from all the other beautiful cups and saucers, but equally beautiful. There were fine-rimmed and fragile cups, as if they were made from something much more delicate than what we would use on a daily basis. They were fragile, dainty and amazingly beautiful, and I knew they were not meant to be used, except at the most special times or events. They were probably not to be touched by anyone, except the proprietress of such a lovely treasure.

There was a gold cup and saucer with bold, deep red lines that circled around them and met at the other end of the line. This beauty, for a long time, graced the marble-top dresser in my bedroom. One day a friend was visiting my home, and I was showing her and her husband around the house. When she eyed the gold with red rings around the teacup and saucer, she said, "I need that!"

At first, I didn't know exactly what she was wanting from amid my treasures, but much to my surprise, it was Grandmother's elegant teacup and saucer sitting in and amongst my beloved belongings. She was sad to hear that it was a prized possession that could not be parted with.

Teatime is me time!

Photo courtesy of *Yvonne Sellers*

There was also a beautiful set of demitasse cups and saucers, with little shamrocks encircling each piece. Actually, they were twice as tall as a demitasse.

Life is like a cup of tea. It's all in how you make it!

– An Old Irish Proverb –

68

Life is like a cup of tea, to be filled to the brim and enjoyed with friends

—Emilie Barnes—

Photo courtesy of *Yvonne Sellers*

Come and share a pot of tea, my home is warm and my friendship is free!

—Emilie Barnes—

Demitasse & Lungo Doppio

Demitasse is French for "half a cup." A demitasse cup typically holds 2 ounces and was used after dinner for espresso and other after-dinner drinks.

There is, in Italian, a taller cup that holds 3 ounces and is known as a lungo doppio or a long double. It was also used for espresso, cappuccino and Turkish coffee after dinner, just as the demitasse cups were used.

Photo courtesy of Yvonne Sellers

o, they may have been or are *lungo doppios* or "long doubles" for the brave in heart who desire that extra ounce of espresso, cappuccino or Turkish coffee. But, whatever their proper name or whatever their function is or was, they were (and still are) very beautiful! Today, one might use them as a beautiful and dainty teacup.

Photo courtesy of *Yvonne Sellers*

Now, who can resist the beauty and charm of a collection of beautiful demitasse cups and saucers that could dress our prettiest tea table? I know I cannot, and so demitasse cups and saucers always have a special place on my tea table, either with clotted cream or a delicious pistachio pudding topped with whipped cream, as you will see in one of my next books—A Southern Lady's Teas.

Andrea McDougal

There were two demitasse cups and saucers, the likes of which I have never seen before or since. One was pink and white, and one was blue and white. They had an art deco flare to them, with little dots attached around the top edge of the cups and around the edge of the saucers. These two little beauties have graced the inside of a charming little white cabinet that has sat on top of a table in my dining room now for forty-two years.

Can anyone ever have too many teacups?

A child's teapot holds
memories of tea parties that
only a child can have.

Andrea McDougal

Tiny little teapots
with pretty little flowers
Are made for little children
with tiny little hands.

Andrea McDougal

My Journey Continues as a Child

"The Little Green House"

Earlier in my journey, I mentioned a green house I loved that was dressed in gladiolas. This is not the same green house. This was a sweet little green house that I loved even more! It was located on the North Shore of New Orleans in a little suburb called Slidell. We were still always in the heart of the city of New Orleans, even though our home was not in the city, simply because we were always visiting family members, and Daddy continued his work in the city.

I suppose I should give a little added information here about New Orleans. To this day, people living on the North Shore still say they are living in New Orleans. But for me, the years spent living in New Orleans were right in the heart of the city and not in a suburb or on the outskirts of the city. That has now changed. During this time, we were on the outskirts of the city, and a very large lake separated us from the heart of the city. Where we were located on the North Shore, when we crossed the lake, Lake Ponchartrain, we would have to drive across a five-mile bridge to get to the heart of the city. For the next five years, there would be many

memories of our goings and comings across that five-mile bridge.

There are other large and growing communities on the North Shore, and from there, the people must cross a twenty-five mile bridge, known as the Causeway, to get to their communities after commuting to and from their jobs in New Orleans.

During our time in the "little green house," it was just Mother, Daddy, myself and my constant companion, my little sister, Lillian. It would be another five years before we would have another addition to our family. I would be nine when our next little sister was born.

I call it the "little green house." Well, of course, it was green. It was the first home my parents would own, a perfect little wooden house with two bedrooms, one bath, a kitchen and a living room. Lillian and I shared a bedroom. I slept in a small bed, and she still slept in her crib.

We had a couple of beautiful pet rabbits, one for each of us, that were allowed to come in the house so we could play with them, and we had a little terrier dog.

This house was one of the first built in that subdivision and was of all new construction. Daddy's sister, Aunt Hazel, and her son lived on that same street about a block before you would get to our home. She had told Daddy about the new starter homes, and he jumped on it as quickly as possible. So here we were living in our own home and no longer renting.

Mother continued to enjoy her special times for afternoon tea while she took time to relax from her housekeeping and cooking. Lillian and I were watching Lassie on TV. Lassie always seemed to be in a dire situation, and Lillian and I couldn't help but shed many tears and become emotionally upset over it. I was still four, and Lillian was only two and a half. It never failed that Daddy would be walking in the door from work just when the most serious moments were taking place in the Lassie saga, and he would find us crying and concerned for Lassie. We were warned, not only by him, but also by Mother, that if we continued to get so upset over a TV show, we would not be able to watch it anymore.

Now, I definitely did not want that to happen, and neither did Lillian. I loved watching Lassie, and I would be very sad without being able to watch that show. So, I was determined not to become so emotional while watching TV. It was a little bit harder for my baby sister, but we had good success.

Some memories are held with paper and glue, and others are held deep in our hearts and minds forever.

Andrea McDougal

Our parents liked to go out to eat and then go dancing. I remember Mother, one evening, coming and sitting on the side of my bed, telling me good night. She said she and Daddy were going out for a while, but they would be home soon. I became very teary eyed, and Mother told me not to be worried or sad, and then she offered me something that soothed my little heart over being separated from them. She promised that every time she would go out with Daddy, she would bring me home something from where they had been. That next morning, when I woke up, on the foot of my bed was a beautiful paper napkin with a pretty design, stating the name of the place they had been, and there was also a matchbook. That was the beginning of my first collection. Soon I was accumulating beautiful paper napkins and a lovely collection of matchbooks.

When Mother asked me if I was enjoying my pretty little gifts, I told her I needed some way to keep them so that the napkins didn't get messed up. She bought me my first scrapbook. I can remember the day I sat on my bed, being just four years old, with my first-ever scrapbook and some paste and began to paste each napkin and matchbook into it, until I had eventually filled every page in my new book of memories.

During the time we lived in the "little green house," I can remember us sitting in our kitchen and Mother preparing us breakfast. We mostly did *not* have cereal, and I was so glad. I was not fond of cereal because I did not like the milk with the wilted cornflakes sitting in it.

I can remember being at Aunt Hazel's house one morning for breakfast. Lillian and I had spent the night there, and oh, how I was dreading breakfast. My cousin, whom we all called Champ and who was several years older than I, loved cereal. When Aunt Hazel asked what we wanted for

breakfast, there was really no option except the dreaded cornflakes in the dreaded milk. I knew exactly the response I was going to get from her, and it was not good. Therefore, I truly tried to drink the milk down with the soggy cereal, but I just couldn't do it.

I tried to get up from the table before she could see me, hoping that just maybe she wouldn't remember that I was the one sitting there. It didn't work, and I had to face the consequence of being called "wasteful."

I do believe my mother spoiled us with her wonderful cooking, and cereal had not become part of her repertoire. Mother would fix us eggs, and we would have either pancakes or waffles. Back then, Lillian loved pancakes, and I loved waffles, and we will leave it at that!

At this sweet "little green house," my grandma and pawpaw would come to visit us. This would be my daddy's mother and stepfather. You have not met her as of yet, but you will soon. If you remember, I would be five before I would meet Grandmother and Grandfather, because they were still living in England during this time. Every time my grandma would come for a visit, she, my Aunt Hazel, and Mother would always have tea together. Now, if it was in the heat of summer, their tea would be iced tea, but tea was always served, either hot or cold!

"I can just imagine myself sitting down at the head of the table and pouring out the tea," said Anne, shutting her eyes ecstatically, "and asking Diana if she takes sugar! I know she doesn't, but of course I'll ask her just as if I didn't know."

– L. M. Montgomery –
Anne of Green Gables

A riddle, wrapped in a mystery, inside an enigma.

— Sir Winston Churchill —

Before we move on to the next house, "our brick house," a very mysterious thing took place. Daddy came into our room early one morning obviously agitated. He came to me first and then to Lillian, who was first sitting in her crib, and then she was standing in her crib. Let me say that the mystery that I am about to share with you was never solved and remains a mystery to my sister and me to this day! Daddy held in his hand a bottle of Vitalis! Some of you may remember what that was, but for those of you who don't, it was a bottle of liquid hair dressing used by men. As Daddy held the bottle up in the air, I could vaguely see something that looked red.

We had just been awakened from a sound sleep, and Daddy proceeded to ask who put the cherries in his bottle of Vitalis. It is so funny to me now, but it was very serious to me then. His bottle of Vitalis was filled with maraschino cherries! We were interrogated back and forth, and I proclaimed over and over, "Daddy, I did not do that!" Lillian, in her tiny little voice, proclaimed, "Daddy, I did not do that."

Daddy finally relented and had to go get ready for work, and to this day the mystery of the maraschino cherries in Daddy's bottle of Vitalis has never been solved.

Who stole the cookies from the cookie jar? Who, me? Not me! Who, me? Not me!

I have often thought about it. I knew I had not done it, but how could a tiny little girl get into the refrigerator, take down the maraschino cherries, get the Vitalis out of the medicine cabinet, open it, and stick all of those cherries into that small bottle, then put the bottle back in the medicine cabinet and the rest of the cherries back in the refrigerator! To me it has always seemed IMPOSSIBLE!

One last thing on the "little green house." I began to be aware of the presence of God! I was still just a little thing and would grow up Methodist, but the Lord would also use the Catholic school that I will tell about in the next chapter.

In my first memory of going to church, I was still four years old, approaching five. Our whole family was attending a service, and Grandma Lillian and some of our other family members were with us. I remember sitting with my parents, Daddy in a suit, Mother dressed so very pretty, and Lillian and I sitting there in dresses that Mother had made. We were all very prim and proper. I do not remember anything else about the service that day, except that the children who were there were given a challenge, or should I say, some homework to do. We had to learn all the verses of Psalm 23 and Psalm 100. Don't ask me how I did it. I am sure that Mother had to help me to learn it all by memory. However it happened, I did it, and those two chapters of scripture have stayed with me all these years.

The Lord is my shepherd; I shall not want.
Psalm 23:1

Make a joyful noise unto the Lord, all ye lands.
Psalm 100:1

We live
by faith
not by sight.

2 Corinthians 5:7

"The Brick House"

This was our second home to purchase, and it had everything a contemporary home could need in the early 1950s. Lillian and I again shared a room, but this time we had the prettiest beds I had ever seen. We each had a beautiful chenille bedspread with lovely chenille flowers. Our headboards were tufted vinyl, and I loved our bedroom!

Our backyard had large pecan trees and a chain-link fence around it because we had a beautiful collie dog named Missy. Missy was the prettiest dog I had ever seen. Her coloring was white with light shades of brown, and she had the sweetest eyes and face.

An opportunity arose for Daddy to get another collie, a male this time. His name was Sir Humphrey, and he was an entirely different-looking collie. Whereas Missy was light colored with a sweet and gentle look about her and in her eyes, Sir Humphrey was much bigger and stronger and had a lot of black in the coloring of his hair. He also had a very different disposition than Missy. So, once we acquired him, we were no longer allowed to play in the backyard as long as he was living with us.

Soon after Sir Humphrey arrived, Missy became pregnant and delivered a beautiful litter of puppies. Mother took care of them and then sold the puppies as they got old enough.

Now, even though we could no longer play in the backyard, it was okay because our front yard became a very beautiful and enchanting place to be. Daddy loved growing things, and soon, at the age of five, I had my first lessons in beautiful plants, shrubs and bushes.

And into the Garden I go to lose my mind and find my soul. —John Muir —

Daddy would come home with the most exotic-looking plants. It was wonderful! Sometimes the plants were bigger than me. Once they began to grow and fill out in the front yard, it truly was like being in a secret garden. I would walk in and amongst these flowering bushes that towered high above me and spread their branches out to the left and right of me and was totally obscure and hidden from any passersby, anyone driving in front of our home or a neighbor to the right or left of us. I was in my own secret garden, totally hidden from the rest of the world.

I watched Daddy plant each one of his treasures, first digging the holes with a post-hole digger, and then using his steady shovel to work the soil. I remember him working so hard to get his prized possessions into the ground that sweat was pouring off of him. He took off his rolled-up short-sleeved shirt and worked in his tank top T-shirt. Mother kept an endless supply of ice tea, with a slice of lemon squeezed into it, for him.

After everything was planted, Mother took me through the garden and told me their names—climbing roses and rose bushes, bottle brush, bridal wreath, azaleas, hydrangeas, Indian hawthorn, camellias and gardenias. So that I would remember them, I would walk in and amongst each plant repeating to myself their proper names. Even though the plants were already big when they were planted, before I knew it, they were as I described them earlier, towering over me and completely concealing me.

My mother would walk with me, telling me the names of each plant, and I was totally amazed and enchanted at what I heard and saw.

Andrea McDougal

Spring had finally arrived, and branches of different plants would be exploding at different times. The names that I was given for the plants in this enchanting, secret garden would now be made clearer for me. I would never forget bridal wreath, with its cascading and long, arched branches filled with cluster after cluster of little white fluffy flowers. When the white of the bridal wreath would rest next to the beautiful fuchsia-colored flowers of the azaleas, the white would make the fuchsia pop. And the Indian hawthorn was there

in the mix. The camellias, by the time spring was approaching, had already been blooming throughout late autumn, winter and early spring and were just fading when the bridal wreath and azaleas were popping out.

The gardenias would make their fragrant display at the end of April and into May. Hydrangeas would begin to bud in late April or early May and their showy flower heads would last for several months into summer, fading at the onset of fall.

A garden that seemed so beautiful, I loved to walk in and amongst the plants, and as they flowered, I would want to never forget their names.

Andrea McDougal

The love of gardening is a seed once sown that never dies.

– Gertrude Jekyl –

And who can forget the showy bottle brush? I loved it when, as an adult, I realized that there were bottle brush trees that were just as showy, so showy that you could identify them from your car when driving by. So, without me being aware of it, I had the beginning of my love of plants and growing things at a very young age. It would stay with me the rest of my life!

Oh my, how could I have forgotten the beautiful and showy caladium bulbs that were planted in the backyard around our pecan trees and would explode into a most prolific display of brightly-colored leaves? They remain a favorite thing for me to grow in my garden to this day!

I especially loved Christmas, as most children do. Mother and Daddy loved Christmas, and so he was always particular about the Christmas tree being decorated just right. The tinsel had to be hung just right. I always loved lying on the floor underneath the Christmas tree and looking up through the branches and seeing all of the lighted, large, colorful Christmas bulbs and the beautiful ornaments.

I remember some of the things I got for Christmas, even at the previous home in New Orleans; for instance, a beautiful bride doll.

You may have noticed that there was no "little" preceding the "brick house." That is because this house had three bedrooms, not just two. It had hardwood floors and a large kitchen and living room. It had a real concrete driveway and a covered concrete carport, and there was a very large utility room or wash room at the end of the carport that Mother said "was every woman's dream."

Sometimes all it takes is a warm cup of
chamomile tea and a hug to make a miracle.

—Amanda McQuade Crawford —

Would you like an adventure now, or
would you like to have your tea first?

— Peter Pan -

bed as a special possession. I loved it so much that I did not want to be separated from it!

There would be many more tea sets with tiny teapots that would grace my area of toys. Some were so tiny and made of something breakable, but others, like this sweet little tin tea set, were so durable that you could do just about anything to them, and they would not break!

I remember being a little older and living in our next home back in the heart of New Orleans, and I had the pieces of my treasured little tin tea set and was still using it. I will introduce that story to you shortly. Lillian and I would play like we were grownups with our cups of imaginary tea. No, I had not yet joined our family "tea-drinking club," but that would come soon.

Two little sisters having tea. Tea for two or two for tea.

A Christmas present that stands out to me at this house was maybe not my first tea set, but it was a tiny tin tea set that I loved. If there was anything really special to me, like a new pair of shoes to go to school, new notebooks for the start of a new school year or a favorite toy, I would always want to sleep with it. Mother would put the item or items, whatever special thing it was, at the foot of my bed, and that was the next best thing to actually sleeping with my new and exciting purchase or gift that I was thrilled about. Well, for the first week that sweet little metal tea set, including its very colorful, cardboard carrying travel box and its real toy teapot, was placed every night at the foot of my

I would now be attending a Catholic parochial school from kindergarten through second grade in Slidell. It was called Our Lady of Lourdes Elementary School. My kindergarten teacher was not a nun, but a regular teacher, and my teachers for first and second grades were nuns—Sister Julianna and Sister Scalastica.

There continued to be old wooden floors for me to look and to walk upon in my very young life growing up. The walk up to our classrooms was on the second floor, which, at that time, was a very large, wide staircase outside made of wood. Then we would cross a threshold from the large outside staircase into a wide open area that led to the right and to the left to our four or more different classrooms. We would experience a new room each year that we were there. All of the floors were dark hardwood floors that I would walk upon daily while in school.

And then there was the sidewalk that led to the front of the church that we would walk on every day to go to church, and I would again walk on the dark hardwood floors that appeared to be as those in other places I had visited that were pivotal in my life.

My parents had decided that the best place for Lillian and me to attend school would be at Our Lady of Lourdes Parochial School in Slidell. With a daily source of godly influence, going to church every day, even though the services were in Latin, walking in and amongst the priests and constantly surrounded by the influence of the nuns who taught us and watched over us, was a good influence.

One of my favorite things was going into the gift shop. It was filled with many beautiful pictures of the Christ and other works of art, both small and large. In that atmosphere, I began to sense a strong call of God upon my life, even in those very young and early years. I would not grow up in the Catholic Church, but in the Methodist Church, but it would be those days among the priests and the nuns and in that spiritual atmosphere that I could sense the presence of God upon my young life, and it would carry me into my purpose and destiny in the Earth.

I am grateful for those young days and the insight my parents had to see what we needed, and I believe they were led by God in their decisions.

He feeds His flock amongst the lilies.

Another Baby Girl
Children bring us a piece of Heaven on Earth

– Roland Leonhardt –

I have now come to my ninth birthday, and in another six weeks, on April 22nd, 1958, another little girl would grace our family, another "lover of everything tea." She would be named Laurel Lee after Grandmother Laurel, Mother's mother. I had been named Andrea Louise for my Great-Grandma Louise, the Mother of Grandma, Daddy's mother, and Lillian Ann had been named after Grandma Lillian, Daddy's mother.

Babies smile in their sleep because they are listening to the whispering of angels.

– Unknown –

But truly God has listened, He has attended to my prayer.

Psalm 66:19

God Hears Our Prayers

I cried unto the Lord with my voice, and he heard me out of his holy hill.

Psalm 3:4

In just a few months we would be leaving our home in Slidell and moving back into the heart of the city. The commuting back and forth to work and home was beginning to wear on our family, and so it was that on Friday, August 15, 1958, we loaded up all our belongings. I was excited. Not only were we moving back to the heart of the city; I would be starting the third grade. I was nine years old, feeling so grown up and full of anticipation, and all those thoughts were delightful to me.

Right before we were about to pull away from our "brick home," I remembered that I was leaving something important behind. I had made sure I had all of my precious possessions, including my scrapbook, but something important to me was not with me. I told everyone to hold up. I had to get out of the car. I had forgotten to get something. It was a succulent plant Grandmother had given to me.

When I was given the very first plant of my own, the only place I could find to grow it without a pot was on the side of the house in some dry and barren soil! I ran to the other side of the house and was able to get what was left of my first experience of growing something on my own. I put it in the car with me and took it to our new home in New Orleans.

It was an extremely hot day in August in New Orleans. If you have ever been to the Deep South during the summer months, you will understand when I say it was a very hot day. Our car was loaded down with us and our belongings, and attached to the car was a trailer carrying Daddy's fishing boat. The boat, too, had been filled with things.

Also, Daddy was driving a small moving truck with all of our furniture, and you might know that the boat trailer had a flat tire on the narrow two-lane, five-mile bridge. I was so concerned at what was taking place. How would we ever make it to New Orleans and get to be in our new home? I presented to Mother numerous questions on what I thought could be great solutions, none of which were of much help.

As I sat in the car with my little siblings (Lillian had just turned eight, but Lee was still a little less than four months old), it was hot, very hot, and we were stranded in the middle of the five-mile bridge over Lake Ponchartrain. Mother had made a container of tea to take with us on the road, and it was a very welcome surprise to each of us to have a refreshing drink to cool us in the oppressive heat.

As I continued to ponder our dilemma, I thought, "We need a miracle." So I simply asked in prayer for a miracle. "Father, we need someone to help us and bring us another tire." Before I knew it, someone drove by, stopped, and was able to replace the flat tire on the trailer. The next thing I knew, Mother was getting back in the car and starting the engine.

Daddy was in the moving truck, so I asked Mother, "What happened?" She said the man who had stopped to help us actually had the exact size trailer tire and was willing to give it to us and put it on the trailer. Daddy paid him something for the tire, and we were now on our way to complete the journey to our new home in New Orleans.

This was amazing to me! I was absolutely astounded by what had just happened. I told Mother that I had just prayed the exact thing, and that God had heard my prayer. She said it was a good thing I had prayed. I thought to myself, "Because a little girl of nine prayed, the God of Heaven and Earth heard her, moved upon her request and made a way where there seemed to be no way."

I cried out to God, and He answered my prayers.

Psalm 120:1

A New Home on Dante Street

I have to say that I loved New Orleans. It was quite the adventure. Now that I was nine, a whole new world was opening up to me, and I felt so very much grown up.

When we drove in front of our new home (not a new house, but a new place for us to live), I saw that it was a traditional two-story New Orleans home with a very wide and large **"pink staircase"** that extended from the sidewalk all the way up to the second floor, and there was a screened-in front porch. Our front door was the door to the left, and what amazed me was that we would also have everything on the street level under that. We called it the basement, but it was not underground.

The front door was glass-paned with two side panels of glass, one to the left and the other to the right of the door, and lace curtains covered both the door and the side panels.

The first room would be our living room, and the next room was separated by lovely French doors (also glass-paned with lace curtains). That probably could have been a formal dining room, but it became my parents' bedroom (because our family had grown).

The next room would be where our newest little sister, Laurel Lee, would sleep and play. There was an extra bed on the other side of the room where Uncle Terry, Mother's brother, would sometimes sleep when he was visiting.

If you have the spirit of a young child, you will never age.

– Dr. Shinichi Suzuki –

Next came a small hall. On the left side of the hall was our bathroom, with a wonderful gas heater that was a very welcome friend in the middle of our colder months.

Then there was our kitchen. It was a very large room, and our table and chairs would sit in the middle of it. This was where a lot of our family fun and creative times would take place. Those times were meant to be to bring about who I would become.

Straight ahead were two doors. The one slightly to the left was a bedroom for Lillian and me. The door to the right was the "spooky door" that led to the "spooky stairs," at the back part of the basement. This was not a door Lillian and I liked to use, and neither did Mother. Just recently I brought up to Mother the proverbial door and stairs. She did not know what words I had used to describe them. Without a nudge from me, she immediately said, "I did not like that 'spooky door' or those 'spooky stairs.' "

When you went through that door, it was very scary. You did not know what would be before you and what might happen to you as you walked down the very dark and gray wooden stairs into an unlit, strange and very "spooky space."

It took me a while to realize that, because the house was so big, we were living in a triplex. We had the whole left side of the very large two-story house, another family had the upstairs only of the right side of the house, and someone else lived in the bottom right side of the house. It was great to have that whole left side of the house, upstairs and downstairs—even though the downstairs was so spooky!

So, here we were. I was nine and going into the third grade, and Lillian was eight and going into the second grade. Once we were enrolled in our new school, Lillian and I would walk every day to school and back. It was only three blocks. These were always such wonderful walks!

A place so beautiful, with houses, gardens, music and dreamy views.

Andrea McDougal

I especially loved seeing each of the other houses along the way. They were each so different, and no two houses were the same. Some had lovely front porches, some were screened in, and others were open-aired. Each house had its own charm and oh, so much character. Some were single-storied houses, and others were two or three stories, but all were full of charm and beauty.

I, of course, loved each garden. Again, each one was different and reflected the personality of its owner. There were always flowers blooming everywhere, depending on the time of year.

We would begin classes at Lafayette Elementary School on Carrolton Avenue. It was four stories high, including the floor level, which housed the cafeteria and auditorium.

Here again, my feet would be walking on hardwood floors and wooden stairs inside the building. The windows to our classrooms were absolutely amazing and beautiful. It was always like being in a giant treehouse with wonderful views everywhere you looked.

It was mostly in my violin classes (that you will soon learn about), while other students were taking their turn to play, that I would have moments in which I could gaze out of those amazing windows that seemed to me to be from the floor to the ceiling. I had the most dreamy and beautiful moments of lingering in another world just meant for me.

It would be here, in New Orleans, at this school and in our home on Dante Street, that I would begin to flourish in the things I now realized I loved to do and was created for.

I know that the most joy in my life has come to me from my violin.

– Albert Einstein –

Soon after starting school, I had the opportunity to learn to play the violin. Both of my parents were thrilled. Daddy even went to speak to my teacher, Mrs. Olsen, to find out if I was a violin prodigy. She assured him that I was a very normal violin student.

I loved music, and I loved playing the violin. It was that Christmas of 1958, at our home on Dante Street, that I got my first violin, and I was elated! I would then be given the most incredible and wonderful opportunity, and that was to play in the Junior Philharmonic Orchestra.

This was a very monumental experience for me. We would practice in our individual schools and at home the parts we would play, and somehow, what seemed to be a massive amount of other students from all of the schools in the New Orleans area would gather together at Dixon Hall in Newcomb College and all play together, with different parts, different notes, different harmonies, and yet we would play as one. There were many sounds, but with every different note blending and flowing together and producing the most perfect and beautiful music.

I was just a small part in the midst of what seemed to be thousands of other children. Our fingers on the violins, violas and every other stringed instrument, with our bows, we produced something of such great beauty, and I got to be a part of it. It was the most amazing feeling that I had felt up to this moment in my life, that there was actually the ability to produce such beautiful sounds, playing different notes and harmonizing, and I was right in the middle of it.

I remember telling Mother soon after this that I had a plan, and I knew exactly what I wanted to do. I would finish at Lafayette Elementary School, I would go on to McMain Junior High School, then on to a specific high school, all with the purpose of going on to a university and playing in their orchestra. *The best laid plans of mice and men … .* Things do not always happen the way we plan them.

Always let your dreams be bigger than your expectations

Andrea McDougal

The fate of a child is in the hands of his parents.

— Dr. Shinichi Suzuki -

At a later time, I told Daddy that I would like to play piano or flute, but he firmly insisted, in fact, he declared, "You will play the violin!" But then, when I was sixteen, he bought me a handmade Martin guitar for Christmas. Mother told me that it normally took six months to a year to get a handmade Martin, but he was able to obtain this one. It was almost miraculous, considering what amazing instruments they were (and still are).

It was an exquisite instrument, and what made it all the more wonderful was that I had now been playing the violin for seven years and was able to teach myself to play the guitar quite well. It would not be until I was twenty-three that I purchased an antique Singer upright piano and I taught myself to play it. I loved playing the piano, and my neighbors loved hearing me play it.

All the years of my playing the violin from the age of nine flowed into a total of forty-one years of playing an instrument Daddy was bent on having me to play. When my children were growing up, I would play the violin at night while they went to sleep, and I would play the violin for most of the rest of my life! Music was always played in our homes when I was a child, especially when we went to bed.

If a musician wants to become a fine artist, he must first become a fine person.

— Dr. Suzuki -

In the lower level of our school was where our cafeteria was located, the classes for the handicapped students and a stage where we would hold special events. One special event I remember: we learned to do a Scottish jig and sang songs about Scotland. Before that, we sang for the school and learned to harmonize. Oh, what joy it was, and oh, so beautiful to my ears and heart. It rang throughout my soul!

I always had a passion for singing, and throughout my life, singing was always there—from elementary school, to junior high and high school, and then in church. I was always in the choir and participated in competitions. As a young adult, in a very fleeting moment, I thought I would have a career in singing. When I had my last child, she was birthed as a song bird, and in those years, her daddy, myself and she would entertain at family gatherings by singing together. Over the years, I wrote several musicals for children's church productions, which were a grand success. One of my young actors grew up to be on Broadway for many years, and he's still there.

New Orleans is known as a party city, and we, as children, were always having the best parties—come-as-you-are parties, Coke parties, birthday parties, LSU/Ole Miss parties. The best party I can remember being invited to was on October 31st, 1959 at the home of my classmate, Tommy Sancton. I arrived at his home early evening. It was much like my home and was on the second floor. The first room I walked into was the living room, where we would be watching one of the most historic LSU/Ole Miss football games. I could see to my left another room with open French doors and a typewriter sitting on a desk. I went into the room, and I could see the branches of trees in the window. I thought, "What a lovely place to write from" (because the beauty of New Orleans was set before me)!

Tommy explained to me that his father was an author. I thought how intriguing this was, and for a moment I wondered what it would be like to be married to an author. Little did I know that one day, not only would I be married to an author, but I would be an author myself. And not only would he be an author; he would also be a book publisher.

That night, Billy Cannon would return a punt for an 89-yard run for a touchdown against Ole Miss. It was an amazing night!

My Special Friends

I believe these friends would go on to accomplish great things in their lives!

I made the best of friends during those days, so that their names stayed with me for the rest of my life. Just to name a few: Beverly Sparkman, Janice Tilton, Susan Keller, Susan Dusang, Diane Gatlin, Gayle Barker, Ronald Palmisano, Charlene Holly, Miriam Dosky, Betsy Sanford, Martha Chin, Tommy Sancton, David Green, Michael Sciortino, Francis LaSalle, Susan Potter, Betty Bohne, Karen Ann Cagle, David Barrios, Andy Bogantes, Ken Bratton, Francis LaSalle, Edward Baar and George Sparfven. Somehow I cannot but help believe that each and every one of these very special people went on to accomplish great things in their lives!

Beverly Sparkman: I remember going to Beverly's home for a visit in the beautiful Fountainbleau Subdivision. We visited in her bedroom that had just been wallpapered with pretty flowers. She thought her room was too small, but I assured her it was very beautiful, that I loved it and that wallpaper makes a room look larger. We had a fun time together, and we played the violin together.

Susan Keller: I would visit Susan's home many times. She lived in a three-story home right on Claiborne Avenue not far from my home off of Carrolton and Claiborne. We had great times together, talking and making plans for things we would like to do.

Ronald Palmisano: I remember Ronald carrying his violin into the classroom, and he was very studious.

Charlene Holly: Charlene and I would sit in patches of clover in her backyard and find clovers with 14 and 16 leaves, which is a real phenomenon. I kept them pressed in my Bible practically my whole life! She told me about the red blown-up throats of lizards being their money sacks. I have a special affinity for lizards and clover. I have actually done drawings of clover. Clover is so beautiful and has such intricate flowers.

Betsy Sanford: Betsy invited me to her family's camp, and we paddled her canoe on their large pond. She told me her family would always go canoing. It was at their camp that I found my turtle I named Esther.

Martha Chin: Martha and I would walk together and visit her parents' Chinese laundry.

Betty Bohne: Betty went with our family on a camping trip on the Pearl River. We camped on a sand bar, swam in the river, watched my parents ski, ate great food and chased away wild boars!

Tommy Sancton: Tommy was a born leader. He was always happy and kind, and he gave the best parties. Going to his home for an LSU/Old Miss game had a great impact on my life and has never left me.

Best friends are never forgotten!

Andrea "Andy" McDougal

A Special Room
for "Make-Believe Tea"

Now, back to our French, New Orleans-style home on Dante Street. Straight ahead were two doors, the one slightly to the left was a bedroom for Lillian and me. The door to the right would be the proverbial door that no one wanted to open, much less go through. It opened to a very narrow and steep set of wooden stairs that were painted gray and led to the back part of the basement. The first room you would get to at the end of the stairs would become my very first tearoom, I just did not know it yet. Mother gave it to Lillian and me to play in.

I immediately began to decorate that room. I found a sofa and pulled together a little table, a rug and other inviting pieces. Lillian and Mother asked me what I was doing. I told them I was fixing a place for us to play and to have company.

I suppose that you know my next move. I found the box with my tea set, and set the table as well as I possibly could.

I did not call it a tearoom then, but now I know what it really was. I can remember telling Lillian, as I was putting the pieces to my tea set out on the table, that we could play like we were having tea and have our new friends over to visit with us. I loved our little room. There was a wooden closet. I opened it up, cleaned it out and fixed it like a china cabinet with all the different things I could put together.

When Mother first saw what I had done, she was surprised and asked, "You did all of this?" She seemed quite impressed. She asked me where I found everything I put into the new-found cabinet. She reminded me that each thing in it belonged to someone else, like my dad, and he would be looking for it. I told her I would tell him what he might be looking for and where he could find it.

I truly loved our little room. I just did not like going through the "spooky door" and down the "spooky stairs" at night. So, I only visited my special room during the day and would drink my "Make Believe Tea."

May all who enter as guests, leave as friends.

Our Kitchen Table
Our fondest memories were made when gathered around the kitchen table.

Our kitchen, in this wonderful shotgun-style home, was the center of fun and learning, and I thought it was all so very wonderful.

At the age of nine, I prepared my first lunch for Lillian and myself in this kitchen. The same day I cleaned the house from the front all the way to the back. I could tell you in great detail how I did it, but you would laugh with amazement at my swift ability. It was so amazing that Daddy told Mother as soon as she walked in the door. I truly never understood why he was in such unbelief at what he saw me doing, until I was an adult, and then I knew exactly why he was amazed. And it was hilarious, what I did to clean the house! I never did it again.

In what seemed to me to be a very large kitchen with large windows that covered the outside wall, we would sit and do the most amazing and wonderful things around the kitchen table!

Home is the starting place of love, hope and dreams

and a cup of "Make-Believe Tea."

Both of my parents were very artistic. Mother, over the years, painted and created many beautiful and wonderful things that each of her girls still own and cherish. Daddy could draw just about anything from memory and then would paint his sketches with beautiful watercolors. I still have two of his paintings in my home.

So here we were in our kitchen at the table. I had also been given my first microscope, and I could spend hours examining everything possible on the glass slides.

Daddy was a very serious coin collector, and he also had a very vast stamp collection that would bring him a considerable amount of money when he eventually decided to relinquish it. I would soon have my own stamp collection in my own book. I still love the beautiful graphics on stamps, so much that I often set them aside in a box to this day. And, to this day, because of my first collection of gifts from my mother of napkins and matchbooks (when living in the "little green house"), I have a passion for the graphics on antique matchboxes.

In this kitchen and around its table we would do crafts, art work, and learn about collecting. All of these days would lead me into my teen years, when I would spend hours drawing, writing, singing, playing the violin or guitar and into my adult years, painting with watercolors. My love for writing and all of the above things would carry me well into my adult life, writing poetry and my Christian teaching books and now this book. So, our lives during those years and even the years ahead were filled with the love of much and the beauty of much.

I would continue in our grand room downstairs, setting my table with my tea set in grand style. During this time, I had acquired a little turtle. I named it Esther, and Esther would make her abode in our little room beyond the "spooky door" and "spooky stairs" that now I know was my pretend and make-believe tearoom. But how could I have given it such a name when I did not know that such a place could exist? I continued to sip my "Make-Believe Tea," as I had seen the women of my family and my mother do in their wonderful ceremony of tea!

Darling, you can have your tearoom now.

– Norton Simon –

Grandma's Beautiful Home on Milan Street

There was so much beauty in mahogany stairs, bamboo shades, chemistry bottles, a stately microscope, cascading plants, antique vases and pots, teapots and teacups, intricately-woven wicker, perfume bottles, art deco coffee pots, a glass biscuit jar filled with cigars, sterling silver and tall glass windows!

I have always loved houses! I love beautiful architecture, houses with charm and character, eye candy, layers, but not clutter, gardens, even if they are green gardens, with different shapes and forms. I say this because I am about to introduce you to one of the favorite houses of my childhood.

For me, every home I lived in was a beautiful and wonderful place to live, but this was not our home. This was my grandma's home. Now, before I can tell you about her home, I must introduce you to my daddy's mother. I knew Grandma right from the beginning of my parents moving back to New Orleans. My memories of her start at her home on Milan Street, that I loved and on to the "little green house," then to the "brick house," on to "Dante Street," and a place I have not mentioned yet.

If you remember, when my parents met, it was because Grandmother, Mother, and Terry were living in a boarding house owned by my grandma, Miss Lillian. At this point, she no longer owned her boarding house, but had become a registered nurse, and was working at Touro Hospital in New Orleans.

Here again, as so many of the houses of New Orleans were, her home was a two-story, New Orleans-style home, and they lived on the second floor. Their home was three blocks off the beautiful and acclaimed Saint Charles Avenue. If you ever get to visit New Orleans, you must not leave there until you have driven up Saint Charles Avenue, or better yet, taken the trolley car ride and seen the exquisite New Orleans-style homes, with massive verandas and very large columns, their moss-hung oak trees that drape from one side of the street to the other, or oak trees

older than most of us, whose branches scoop down to the ground and kiss the grass. Many of those branches I have sat upon and played as a little girl.

Let us not forget the glorious gardens! Spring brought rich colors of wisteria, lingering camellias, roses, gardenias and an explosion of fuchsia, pink, white and red azaleas, accented by dogwood trees and cascades of white bridal wreath. Then came masses of large and showy hydrangeas with a profusion of blues and pinks.

At the closing of spring, when summer was fast approaching, there would be

the beautiful southern mimosa tree, as it dressed itself in fluffy, pink flowers. And how could we forget the color-drenched crepe myrtles of pink, white and red, a beautiful gift from above that brings so much beauty to our eyes when the heat of summer seems so oppressive?

You will see Loyola University, and right next door is Tulane University, and across the street from there will be the very old and beautiful Audubon Zoo. You should even visit the streets off of Saint Charles Avenue. The charm and beauty of those homes and streets are just as enchanting as Saint Charles Avenue. In fact, the rest of the streets, homes and gardens throughout the city are equally filled with history, charm and beauty.

My first memory of visiting Grandma's home was at the age of two, when we had moved back to New Orleans after my dad had finished his schooling. We parked on the side of her home on Milan Street. It was a very grand-sized home and was on the corner of Milan and another street. It was owned by an older lady who lived on the bottom floor.

We walked up a few concrete stairs, and there were two very beautiful doors, both with leaded glass designs and lace curtains veiling what was on the other side of them. The door to the left we would never enter into, for this was the entrance for the owner of this lovely, quaint and charming home.

Then there was the door to the right. First, Mother would ring the doorbell, and the door would unlock, and then Mother opened the door, which was to take us to the second floor of the house. Then, right before my eyes, there was what seemed, to me, to be a very large staircase. I know the stairs were steep because I thought, "How can I step up to the next step without falling off." My little legs had not reached a height yet that would make it possible for me to go up the stairs with ease.

As before, with every pivotal moment and place in my life, the stairs were wood — solid, deep, dark mahogany stairs, and never (no, not ever) would you have found a speck of dust or hair or anything else on them. They were always spotless and shiny.

Mother was holding Lillian, and so I led the way, trying to hold on to the banister and stretch each leg as much as I possibly could to get up the stairs. Eventually, I had to resort to climbing the stairs on hands and knees. We made it to the top, and there was a whole other world that would be before my eyes.

First, there was a very tiny bedroom to the right that I remember sleeping in when we were visiting and it was late at night. The next room to see was Grandma's kitchen, where we would sit at her table. She would always offer a cup of coffee and chicory to my parents or a hot cup of tea or iced tea on very hot days. She would always offer to cook something for us to eat, which I can assure you was always unbelievably delicious. It would be from my grandma that I would learn to cook her recipe for eggs, scrambled with chopped onions, bell peppers and either sausage or bacon. And she could cook the most amazing scrambled eggs. They simply filled the pan, and she would flip them solid, and they had the most incredible light brown texture on both sides and the most delicious taste to them. Oh, how I tried over the years to get that same light brown texture on both sides and that same flavor. I have only a couple of times achieved it.

There was a bedroom to the left of the kitchen at the back of the house. It was beautifully decorated and had a very ornate fireplace opposite the bed. This was where Grandma kept her the dolls she had from the time of her childhood. There were beautiful bisque, perfectly-dressed dolls in their original bonnets and gowns or dresses with lace trims, all perfect as if they were still new. Two rested their heads on the pillows of the perfectly made bed. One was lying in its own wooden cradle that would rock back and forth, and another little boy doll dressed in light blue pants and cap sat in his own highchair.

Grandma was giving me a tour of her very intriguing and beautiful home. She showed it to me room by room. In this particular room, I was given two very strict instructions: One was to never pick up or touch her dolls. They were very delicate and incredibly old. The other came as we approached the other side of the room. There were beautiful drapes that matched the fabric on the bed, and they dressed the largest windows I had ever seen. Her instruction, at this point, was to never open the windows and to stay far away from them at all times. She didn't want us falling out.

There were two brass plates at the bottom of the windows where you would put your hands to raise them. Her concern was the windows started almost at floor level and went what seemed to me to be to the ceiling. Even though this was the second story of the house, there were ten-foot-tall ceilings. She opened one of the windows for me to see out, and there were no screens. If we were to open them, we could fall out. I could see all the way to the sidewalk, where our car was parked.

I noticed the texture of the glass (if you can call it a texture). It was antique glass that had a very different appearance from the smooth window glass of today, and it was quite beautiful.

We then walked through a door into another bedroom, which was hers and my Papaw Leslie's bedroom. The thing I remember about this bedroom was her dressing vanity to the left of the room. It was filled with bottles of perfume, a makeup drawer and pretty containers of face powder and rouge. There were clear ornate glass boxes that held some of her jewelry. This is where she would sit to put on her makeup and to dress in her white nurse's uniform, with white stockings and white shoes. The final part to her dressing was to take two bobby pins and pin her white nurses' hat to her graying hair.

The next rooms were amazing to me, so beautiful that I have never forgotten them. We were back in the hall, passing up the grand mahogany staircase, and now going into the rest of the house. The room to the left was a very large dining room with a perfectly polished (here again) mahogany dining room table that seemed to seat eight to ten people, and that it did. We would eat many fancy and delicious meals there as little girls.

There was a matching china cabinet filled with many splendid pieces of beautiful china for special occasions, with matching teacups, saucers and teapots that intrigued me. There was also a buffet table Grandma served from.

As I looked straight ahead and a little past this dining area, there was the most amazing room I could only get a glimpse into. There were glass French doors that were closed and were soon opened by Grandma. And there were bamboo shades over screened windows, different from the floor-to-ceiling windows, and there was shelf after shelf filled with the most amazing and massive collection of bottles, with glass-knobbed stoppers or lids. There were also plants cascading off the shelves and a desk and chair, with a very old, black typewriter sitting on

a wooden desk. There was also a microscope, something I had never seen before (this was before the age when I was given my own microscope on Dante Street). I loved this little room that was filled with a beauty I had never before seen.

Next, to the right of the dining room, was a large living room with antique pots and figurines on tables with marble tops and marble pillars and iron figurines, and the most intricate wicker pieces that still stand out in my mind. I had never seen the like of them before and have never seen the likes of them since. There was also another fireplace. Its mantle was dressed in more collectibles.

Looking in the same direction, but off of the living room, was another room at the front of the house with French doors just like the room off of the dining room. I was told that these two little rooms, both filled with beauty, but a different beauty, were porches off the front of the house. The one by the China and flower-filled dining room was for Papaw Leslie, and the other one was for Grandma. It contained her intricately woven wicker furniture and ferns and palm plants sitting in lovely old pots perched on plant stands.

I soon learned that Papaw Leslie was a chemist for the State of Louisiana, and his porch was his office. In front of his bamboo shades and cascading plants were shelves filled with such beautiful bottles with large shapes in shades of blues and browns and clear glass. These were his chemistry bottles. This was definitely one of my favorite houses to visit.

A Preliminary to Officially Joining Our Tea-Drinking Club

I had a tiny taste of tea in a tiny little cup.
It' was a memory that stayed with me forever!

Andrea McDougal

My time to officially join our generations of tea drinkers and to become a part of our "tea-drinking club" was fast approaching. Although, I must confess, I did have a preliminary experience! This would take place when I was nine years old at my grandma's home. Now, neither Grandma nor I was aware of our official "tea-drinking club," but I did officially become a "tea drinker" at the age of twelve and joined the club of our generations of "tea drinkers." Somehow that age seems to be the perfect time, or should I say the "coming of age" for the official beginning of a "tea-drinker's life."

My story begins at Grandma's home, the house in which every room had a rich taste of beauty. As I mentioned, this first taste of tea was at the age of nine. This was the time that we had moved back to New Orleans on Dante Street.

There had been many visits up until this point, but this time Grandma was preparing a pot of tea for Papaw Leslie to have in his chemistry office. So that he would have a generous portion to last him awhile, she poured his tea into a lovely art deco coffee pot and left the teapot full for herself. She asked me if I would like to have a taste of tea with her.

Mother had asked Grandma if I could stay with her for a couple of hours while she would take my little sister, Lillian, to a dental appointment. Grandma would soon be getting dressed for her shift at the hospital, and Mother had promised not to be long. Grandma took one of the art deco demitasse cups and saucers that went with her art deco coffee pot and poured the slightest bit of tea into my soon-to-be first taste of tea, then added a tiny spoon of sugar and a little milk. I would say the tiny cup was about half full of tea and the other half, with warm milk. She took the tiny golden spoon and stirred my cup and placed it before me as we sat at her dining table.

A taste of tea that warmed my belly.

Andrea McDougal

Please come, you are invited for a cup of tea. Won't you come on in!

Andrea McDougal

I sat there watching the tiny swirl of heat go up out of the cup and admiring the beauty of what was set before me. I slowly began to take the tiniest taste of the first bit of tea to wash over my tongue. I drank it ever so slowly with a little trepidation, not knowing at all what to expect.

The tiny cup was so very thin and fragile. I had never held anything so delicate before. My lips were perched upon the cup in a way I had also never experienced before. My first taste of tea was oh, so grand, but I would not drink a cup of tea again until I was twelve and would officially become a "tea drinker" for the rest of my life and would join our family's "tea-drinking club!"

Complimentary colors of blues and yellow. What a glorious combination in art deco style! Comfy pillows and large white spider lilies from the garden! A fragrance that mingled with the slightest hint of Earl Grey tea!

Andrea McDougal

117

Learning to drink and enjoy tea was a gift my mother gave me.

Andrea McDougal

When you introduce someone to tea, it will remain with them for the rest of their life. *Andrea McDougal*

My Time Had Come to Join Our Tea-Drinking Club

*"Yes, that's it!" said the Hatter with a sigh.
"It's always teatime."*

Lewis Carroll, Alice in Wonderland

Yes, the official moment in time had come when I would join the "family tea-drinking club!" I was now at the approximate age of twelve. As I thought back on this monumental moment in my life, I thought how apropos it would have been to have joined our proverbial "tea-drinking club" exactly where my mother had her first cup of tea and among all of the matriarchs of our family.

I know you will remember the lovely green house in New Orleans that was so beautifully dressed in an array of colors from Great-Aunt Helen's gladiolas. This was the scene of Mother's first cup of tea. This was also the home where I ate my first piece of King Cake, and I, of all the people there getting a slice of a delicious Mardi Gras cake, would get the "little baby" when I bit into my slice. Aunt Helen had declared that whoever got the baby would have to host the next King Cake party. I was mortified! I turned to my mother with the tiny plastic baby in my hand and immediately asked her, "How will I do a King Cake party?" She told me not to worry about it and declared me the winner, having received the tiny plastic baby in my slice of cake.

This home that I loved so much would also be where we sat around the table, and I would learn to do my first piece of embroidery on a light blue table scarf (that I still have in my possession to this day). This house would be where my cousins and I would dance and play and have so much fun. But even though it seemed to be the perfect place, in my mind, in retrospect, it could never be because Aunt Helen died very young. She was only thirty-eight, and I was five. She passed away suddenly around the same time that Ma Mére left us. I never got to tell you that she was also my God-Mother. It just was not meant to be that I would be in the midst of those who had gone before me, but it was still oh, so grand in my eyes.

Now, you do realize that at the perfectly-ordered moment of my becoming a lifelong tea drinker, I did not know that I was joining anything, and I did not know that I had come to the age of having tea. Well, maybe I did realize that, but the rest remained a mystery ... until all the pieces of the puzzle finally came together.

Experiencing your first cup of tea lets you know you have begun to grow up, and a whole new world is beginning to open up to you.

Andrea McDougal

Happy Birthday to you!
Happy Birthday, dear Andy!.
Happy Birthday to you!

It was March 10th, 1961, and it was my twelfth birthday. I had been to school and had just arrived home. We were still living on Dante Street. My heart was a tad bit heavy because it seemed like no one had remembered my birthday. Then Mother called me into the living room. "Andy, come here," she said. "I need to talk to you." To me, she sounded so serious.

As we sat on the sofa, she began to tell me that she was not going to be able to do anything for my birthday because that year things were too tight financially. She continued by telling me that she had something special for me. "Because you are my first-born daughter, I want to give you something that has been in our family for many generations. It was worn

Perfectly wonderful and loving gifts!

by your great-grandmother, Mére, your grandmother, Laurel, and many other women. It is incredibly old and has been passed down through many generations." Then she opened something wrapped in soft paper and unveiled a beautiful and very delicate watch. I had never seen anything like it before or since. It was very tiny and delicate.

The watch itself was sterling silver. The face had Roman numerals and very ornate clock hands. There were six diamonds on the top of the watch face and six diamonds on the bottom of the watch face. The bracelet part was made of black cord that would loop around into an opening at the top of the watch and another black cord that would do the same at the bottom of the watch. The two ends

from the top would clamp into one part of the latch that would close and keep the watch on your wrist, and the other two ends of cord would be clamped into the other part of the latch. I have treasured that watch since the day she gave it to me, and I wore it every chance I got. I absolutely loved my watch.

Mother also gave me a gold monogrammed ring. It was her graduation ring from high school. I have cherished and worn that ring throughout life!

That day Mother said to me, "I hope you understand and that you like my special gifts for you." I answered, "Of course. It's a beautiful gift, and I love each piece." I asked her if Daddy knew. She said he did and agreed that I should have her special gifts.

Well, at this point, I knew I was twelve. I remember telling you how I felt at the age of nine, but maybe not as strongly as I should have. Nine was like an explosion of life, being grown up and expecting everything wonderful to make its way to me and inside of me. But now I was twelve, almost a teenager.

I have always lived with an expectancy of great and new things every day of my life. I suppose it was innately birthed inside of me by God Himself. The next thing I knew, Mother said, "Would you like to have a cup of tea with me?"

God is love, and
he who abides
in love abides
in God, and
God in him.

1 John 4:16

Oh, my! Here it begins! A journey I was not aware that I was on takes a leap and carries me through to this day. I responded without hesitation, "I would love to have a cup of tea with you!" We made our way to the kitchen, and Mother pulled out of the cabinet two very lovely cups, both different. She put the kettle on our gas range and lit the fire, and we waited to hear the whistle.

My teacup and saucer had beautiful pink flowers on it. I do not know if the flowers were moss roses or strawberry flowers or what they were. All I know is that my tea tasted oh, so good in such a lovely cup. I later learned that it was a Royal Albert teacup and saucer that had been gifted to her.

I had to ask how to fix my tea, and Mother told me, "First, put a teabag in your cup, and when the kettle whistles, very cautiously we will pour the water into our cups. But be sure to leave some room for the milk. We will let the teabags sit in our teacups for three to five minutes, which is called 'letting the teabag steep,' and then we will take our teabags out and squeeze them, pressing them against our spoon to get the last bit of tea out of the bag. I usually add two teaspoons of sugar, stir it, and then I add some milk to top it off."

I did all that she said, and then came my first sip of tea since I was nine. You do remember my preliminary tiny taste of tea at the age of nine? This was different! I was twelve, and it was my birthday, and I was drinking tea with the woman in my life who meant everything to me—Mother. It was a wonderful experience. I loved the taste of tea, and I had a very pretty teacup and saucer to drink it from. I loved it all. I just did not know it was taking me on a journey of "loving everything tea" and "everything beautiful." I am so happy that it did.

To top it off, we fixed the most delicious grilled-cheese sandwiches. They tasted absolutely perfect with our tea, and then we shared a delicious, freshly-made chocolate éclair from our neighborhood bakery. The whole experience was delightful! Without knowing it or having any inkling of it, I had officially joined our family's "tea-drinking club!"

A thoughtful and loving Mother who made my twelfth birthday memorable and magical without even knowing it!

Andrea McDougal

A White Dress with a Red Sash
and a cup of "Victory Tea"

So, here I am, twelve years of age, It is now May of 1961, and I have just graduated from the fifth grade at Lafayette Elementary School. In fact, we had a wonderful graduation. All the girls had to wear white dresses for the graduation and our party afterwards, where we would get to dance. I can remember having a conversation with my teacher about why we would be dancing with boys. She was very kind as she told me that now we were getting older, we had just accomplished six years of school (if you count Kindergarten), and now it was time for us to learn how to dance with boys, and for the boys to learn how to dance with us. So, now she was teaching us and practicing with us on how we should dance with each other, since after the graduation ceremony, we would be having a party, and there would be dancing, boys with girls and girls with boys.

The search for a dress that could not be found.

Andrea McDougal

Mother and I searched everywhere for a solid white dress. We did find a very pretty white dress, with one simple little problem. The dress was white, but it had a large red satin ribbon that went around the waist and tied in a bow! Oh, how I fretted over that red ribbon and its big red bow at the back!

I appreciated Mother finding me such a pretty white dress. In fact, it was white eyelet with its own slip underneath. But it was not solid white, and I would be the only girl there with a red satin ribbon tied around my waist and a noticeably big bow in the back. I fretted!

Even though we danced all the time at home, and it always looked just right, I can remember when it came to dancing with a boy or boys at our graduation party. Everything seemed so stiff, awkward and a little scary, yet fun!

When I arrived home, Mother asked how things worked out with my white dress and red satin ribbon, Much to my surprise, I was not distressed at all about it. I was able to tell her that it was great. Everyone had loved my dress, and no one had said anything about it having a big satin red ribbon around my waist.

Then we sat down and had a cup of what I call today "Victory Tea." All my fretting had been in vain. Red sash and all, everything had been absolutely grand!

My fretting had been in vain!
Everything had been absolutely grand!
A cup of "Victory Tea," please! Andrea McDougal

128

Love conquers all!

The Neighborhoods of
New Orleans

A neighborhood is for experiencing life, making friends and memories.

Andrea McDougal

I have loved every home, every neighborhood that has been part of my life, each one being different, with its own charm and beauty, yet there is something very special about New Orleans neighborhoods.

If you were to divide New Orleans up into its individual neighborhoods, there would be a multitude of grocery stores, bakeries, restaurants, cleaners, shoe repair shops, churches and anything else of necessity.

Living in a New Orleans neighborhood with all its charm and beauty was like living in a storybook.

Andrea McDougal

I loved the fact that we could take a casual walk up the street or across the street, and there would be a grocery store or whatever we needed. If not, then you could easily catch a trolley car, whose wheels would click and clack against its railway tracks and whose bell would ring every time someone needed to get on or off.

Neighborhoods in New Orleans remain much the same today. Every little neighborhood, spread out over a few square blocks, seemingly has its own grocery store, bakery and other places of necessity. I can remember, as a young girl, the shoemaker's repair shop. Oh, how enchanting it was for me to get a glimpse into another world of the shoe repairman's shop—the smells, the sounds and the hard work that went on in the tiny but effective little shop. It was all imprinted in my memory.

There was even a Chinese laundry owned by the Chin family. Their daughter was a classmate that I had the opportunity to spend much time with. Not only were we in the same classes for a few years, but we also learned to play the violin together, along with our other classmates.

So many walks were taken daily for a loaf of bread or a box of tea. Beans were taken from a barrel and put into a brown paper bag and then weighed.

My greatest lessons about food were taught to me by my mother, when we were at our neighborhood grocery store. There I learned the difference between bananas and plantains, that an avocado was also known as an alligator pear. I learned a lot about meat as we watched the butcher cut our meat and learned of the lesser qualities of meat that would be used in certain dishes, such as ham bones, cuts of beef, *et cetera*. And I learned that tea came in two different ways: loose tea and tea bags.

And now, there will be a new neighborhood that I will love and find to be endearing.

Andrea McDougal

Won't You Be My Neighbor?

It's a beautiful day in this neighborhood,
A beautiful day for a neighbor.
Would you be mine?
Could you be mine?

I have always wanted to have a neighbor just
like you.
I've always wanted to live in a neighborhood
with you.
So, let's make the most of this beautiful day,
Since we're together, we might as well say,
Would you be mine?
Could you be mine?
Won't you be my neighbor?
Won't you please,
Won't you please?
Please, won't you be my neighbor?

– Fred Rogers –

Saint Mary Street

Another place, another home, with many adventures and memories to keep with me.

Andrea McDougal

Home is where the heart is!

Major changes would be taking place in my life and in the lives of my family members. We would once again be moving, this time to a place I had not known of before. My dad was wanting to open his own business, and so that was what our next adventure would be. We were now moving, not too far from New Orleans, to a small community called Thibodaux.

I would begin my new school year, Junior High School, in this very quaint and charming town, where you could walk everywhere you wanted to go, including the neighborhood grocery store, school, department stores and even church—if your heart so desired.

No one in Thibodaux sounded like us, for it was a very French community where most people were French Acadians or Cajuns. When we were standing in line at school, the other students would ask me to say something, just anything, so they could hear how I sounded, how I pronounced my words.

I did not sound like them when I spoke because I was a New Orleans girl, a city girl.

We would, once again, be living in a two-story home, and there were two bedrooms upstairs in a converted attic. I would now have my own bedroom, and Lillian and Laurel Lee would share the other bedroom. I realize now why they have, to this day, a very close friendship.

I loved my bedroom. My bed fit so perfectly within a cubby area, with the head of the bed against two windows that looked out over a terribly busy two-lane street. Mother gave me a genuinely nice portable sofa that could fold down for company to sleep on. It was mid-century, contemporary and a lovely burnt orange color.

There was also another piece of furniture that I loved very much. It was a very wonderful narrow bookcase to store my books and collectibles on. Mother told me it was Daddy's bookcase but that he said I could have it. It was not plain and simple. The sides of it, at the base of the first shelf, to the top, was a beautiful openly cut-out design that was very ornate and quite lovely.

This room became a sanctuary for me, a place where I would write stories and poetry. I would draw for hours—horses, flowers and the faces of people. I loved to sing, so I would sing. When Daddy gave me the Martin guitar, I would play it and sing. I would practice singing because now I was in the choir at school and also at my new Methodist church.

I have come to realize that many keys are given to us over the years, and keys are made for unlocking doors!

Andrea McDougal

I loved playing the violin.

It was like the bow, the violin, the notes of the music and I would become one, as I played my instrument.

Andrea McDougal

I would practice playing the violin for hours. My parents would be finding me a new private violin teacher. There would be no orchestra or stringed instruments at our public schools, only band and choir. I had to play the violin in a recital, and I was the only violin student. My photograph was taken by the Thibodaux newspaper, "The Comet," and it was written in the article that I was the only violin student in the city of Thibodaux or any of the surrounding communities, and they needed to have an orchestra with stringed instruments in their school system. Now, years later, they have an orchestra and children go to school with their violins, violas, cellos and maybe a base fiddle or two!

Music brings healing to the soul!

Even though Mother would be helping Daddy to start their first business, keeping house and cooking wonderfully delicious meals, somehow she found time to make Lillian and me new dresses to start school with, just as she had done for our school years in New Orleans. I absolutely loved the dresses she made for me and wish I still had them. I can remember the styles and even the fabrics she used. All were so stylish and cute.

It would be at this age of twelve, after so many years of watching Mother make our clothes, that I began to make many of my own clothes. Laurel Lee, whom we have always called Lee, was now three years old, and I'm sure Mother also made her clothes, along with mine and Lillian's.

I was to find great favor with my teachers in this new place and loved going to school. Once we began high school, Lillian and I would sometimes ride the bus to and from school. Or we could walk there and back, probably about two miles each way.

I also loved going to the Methodist church and being in the choir there. Mother would take me and pick me up. Or, if the weather was really nice, I would walk a couple of miles there and back. I must say that on my walks to and from school or to and from church or to and from wherever I was going at the moment, I had some great adventures. Those adventures will have to be for another time and another book. Now, it's teatime.

Since officially joining our family "tea-drinking club" on my birthday while living at Dante Street, my breakfast before school now consisted of a cup of hot tea and toast. Sometimes I ate something else, but I always had a cup of tea.

Then, when we would arrive back home from school, we would always have a snack. This might be a couple of pieces of toast and a cup of hot tea. I remember sitting at our kitchen table one day. Mother was at one end of the table, close to where I would normally sit, and I was sitting where Daddy would always sit. We were drinking our afternoon tea with toast and so enjoying our time together. Mother looked at me, smiled and said, "There is nothing like a cup of hot tea and toast," and I agreed with her wholeheartedly!

"A cup of hot tea and toast,"

I agreed wholeheartedly!

Andrea McDougal

Music acts like a magic key to which the most tightly closed heart opens!

– Maria Von Trapp –

My Tea Journey Continues

Mother's Garden and a Cup of "Sweet Pea Tea"

Love is the garden of my soul!

In search of my mother's garden, I found my own.

—Alice Walker—

This would be the first garden that was only Mother's, and I loved it! I had never known a garden like hers before. Yes, my dad planted many plants, and they were always incredibly beautiful and wonderful. His gardens impacted my life and were enchanting to me.

Daddy would also have a very productive vegetable garden for many years, and Great-Uncle Truman had the greatest vegetable garden, so tall and beautiful that I was safe inside of it. And, of course, there was Aunt Helen's bed of gladiolus. But Mother's garden was different.

I remember the day I came home from school, and the whole side of the fence,

from the front of the driveway, all the way to the end of the backyard, was freshly dug for a flower bed. Daddy had rented a tiller to till his vegetable garden at the back of the yard, and he had tilled this massive flower bed and another garden bed around the back porch.

I had walked home from school that day, and when I walked into the yard and saw this freshly-tilled earth and Mother working in the soil, I was elated. I was so excited for Mother and her garden, and I think I was also excited about the outcome—without knowing the end result. I also think I was excited, knowing somehow that this garden would bring us joy, and that it did.

I watched Mother sow her seeds. One by one she would place them in the soil. She even rolled out fibered paper that already had seeds in the fiber, and all you had to do was to roll it on top of the soil, water it and watch your plants begin to spring up and produce beautiful flowers. It was absolutely amazing to me that such a wonderful thing existed. I was totally enthralled with every detail, from beginning to end.

I believe that while we were in our last few days of school for that year, Daddy would take Mother to pick out her seeds and the roll-out fiber to put into her garden. Every day, when I got home from school, there was something new for me to see and to hear about.

I was always very inquisitive, and I wanted to know the name of every seed she was planting and what it would produce. She obliged me, telling me some of the names of the flower seeds. Some were new to her, and she was just as excited for them to spring up and grow and produce their blossoms and to see the fruit of her labor as I was.

Every day, when I got home from school, I would immediately walk up and down her flower beds, looking for new little blades that had sprung up. Eventually those little blades would become lush, flowering plants. This was always the first thing I would do—even before my afternoon cup of tea.

Then summer vacation had come, and I would be at home through each day, watching and waiting for Mother's flowers to bloom. There were zinnias, bachelor buttons, marigolds, daisies, coreopsis, cosmos, morning glories, calendulas, gomphrena, coleus and others I cannot recall.

Since summer was trying to break through, our afternoon tea became iced tea. It was so delicious, and we absolutely had to have sugar and lemons, and each glass was individually made just right. We would drink our tea, walking up and down the flower beds, enjoying the brilliant display. I was even compelled to do a drawing or painting of zinnias that almost looked like a Van Gogh sunflower painting.

My cup of tea amongst the sweet peas was oh, so grand!

Andrea McDougal

If you remember, I mentioned the tilled bed around the back porch. This became an oh, so enchanting place for me.

Then, all too soon, summer came to an end, and fall and winter would be upon us. Mother did something so wonderful and beautiful, something I loved and would never forget. When it was still winter (with no sign of spring before us), she planted around the back porch seeds of the glorious, beautiful and fragrant sweet pea. Once they began to come up, she took string and made a wall of string that her sweet peas would eventually climb up. The string was nailed beneath the floor of the porch on the outside edge and extended to a top support, along both front and side of the open porch.

In time, the tendrils of the sweet peas climbed from the floor to the ceiling, forming two walls of vine-covered string from the floor to the roof of the porch. Every inch of space was covered. I remember one Saturday it was raining softly, but that was outside of my very protected closed-in, walled-in porch of sweet peas. I could not see out into the yard.

It was morning, and we were getting ready to go to Jena to see my favorite cousins, the Fluitts. I would normally have had my tea in the kitchen or taken it upstairs with me to my bedroom, but that day, I walked out the back door with my wonderful cup of hot black tea and sat there in an unassuming chair before a very small and equally unassuming table, where I placed my freshly-made cup of hot tea. Suddenly I found myself enclosed in a very whimsical land of the sweetest fragrance, with beautiful candy-colored flowers all around, and the rain was lightly falling upon the leaves and the flower petals, and the mist from the drops of rain would hit my skin. It was all so magical to me. It was like I had become a character in a beautiful fairytale or story about a magical garden.

Mother called for me to hurry, but all I wanted to do was to linger in this place I had never seen before. I answered back, telling her I was in the land of sweet peas, drinking my cup of "Sweet Pea Tea." There was a joy inside of me as she tried to hurry me, and I explained that I was so incredibly loving where I was in those moments.

"Aren't you getting wet?" she asked. "I am far enough away," I answered, "that I am not getting wet." It was technically a little fib. There were a few splatterings from off the leaves, as it suddenly began to rain much harder. To this day, I love a garden that is taller than me and makes me feel surrounded by its beauty! I loved sipping my "Sweet Pea Tea."

Two Baby Girls

Babies are a gift from God!

Let her sleep, for when she wakes, she will move mountains."
– Napoleon Bonaparte –

In writing this book, so many things have been made clear to me. I now realize that while we were still living in New Orleans on Dante Street, in my birthday month of March, when I was twelve, Mother conceived another daughter who would grace our family and bring a lot of joy and delight along with her. Nine months later, on December 6th, 1961, a little sister by the name of Yvonne Marie would enter our world. And what a delight she was!

Yvonne was an exceptionally happy and wonderful child, just as Laurel Lee was. They both should have been called "Joy."

Four years later, the last of our girls would be born into the family. So, in 1965, when I was fifteen, on February 16th, our youngest sister came into our world—Lynn Adair. In just a few short weeks, I would be sixteen. Lynn would be the last of Mother's girls. And, Lynn, just as Lillian, Laurel and Yvonne, brought so much joy and happiness into our family. No wonder Daddy called her "Precious Jewel"!

My Sisters

Because I have a sister, I will always have a friend!

Daddy loved taking photos of his girls, but especially his baby girls, Laurel Lee, Yvonne Marie and Lynn Adair. His eyes would glisten as he would take photos of his little ladies, and they would always give him joy, laughter and the absolute cutest photos! Daddy's girls gave him so much happiness, and his heart for them would shine through his eyes, like glistening diamonds. Mother and Daddy adored each of us girls and knew we would do great things.

Sisters make the best friends in the world.

– Marilyn Monroe –

When our hearts are broken, it is a sister that helps to hold

us together

Andrea McDougal

In the cookies of life, sisters are the chocolate chips.

– Unknown –

Each of these girls in our family—Lillian Ann, Laurel Lee, Yvonne Marie and Lynn Adair—were little beauties, and they still are. All are highly creative, artistic, business wise, spiffy dressers, great decorators of their homes and have been excellent mothers to their children! And you will be happy to know that they all joined our family's "tea-drinking club," making them all "tea drinkers" and "lovers of everything tea." They each love beautiful teacups, saucers and teapots and are "lovers of everything beautiful!" And whenever I visit one of their homes, I am always offered a cup of hot tea!

A loyal sister is worth a thousand friends!

146

Above all, clothe yourselves with love, which binds us all together in perfect harmony.

Colossians 3:14

Whoever does not love does not know God, because God is love

1 John 4:8

My Last Summer Visit with Grandmother

A Cup of "Reward Tea"

This would be my last summer to spend at Grandmother's home on the Gulf Coast. I had just finished my junior year of high school. This year I would be going to Grandmother's by myself. Lillian would not be going this time, so it was the Greyhound Bus, there and back, for me.

My first full day at Grandmother's, I would be helping her by cleaning the leaves on two of the very large plants in her foyer. One was a larger-than-me schefflera, and the other was a taller-than-me rubber tree. I was very diligent in getting every leaf clean, including the top of the leaf and the underside.

By the time I had struggled on the floor and behind the plants, reaching to the top branches of her schefflera and then moved on to the rubber tree plant, maneuvering my body, I was exhausted! I was even a little out of breath.

I tell you this little memory because just some days ago, in our home, I was cleaning the leaves of my large schefflera and rubber tree. I was doing the exact thing I was doing as a teenager at Grandmother's, and honestly, I felt the exact same way I felt that morning. I felt the same way now in my own home, cleaning the leaves of my giant schefflera and rubber tree plant in the foyer.

Why did I share this with you? Mostly because I was going somewhere with my story, for there is an outcome that delighted me. But it is to say to you that the total of my life, the things I felt as a little girl are the same feelings and emotions that I have as an adult. I am who

I was as a little girl, the same as I am today. Yes, we grow and mature, we change, we have much more knowledge and, hopefully, more wisdom, and we grow in the knowledge of the Lord, but we are who God made us to be in the beginning, and life molds and bends us into a better type of who we were as a child.

Now, what was the delightful outcome? Grandmother was very pleased with the job I had done on her plants. I even passed the dust mop over the foyer floor. So, she called me into the kitchen, and there was her teapot sitting on the kitchen counter and a teacup prepared just for me with black tea and a full slice of lemon. The kettle was on the stove and began to whistle.

On a saucer was my favorite addition to a cup of tea, a slice of dark rye bread with a spread of blue cheese and a slice of tomato on top. What a delight for me! And a cup of "Reward Tea."

What Is a Pantry

Pantry: a storeroom, a chamber, a cabinet or a closet used for the storage of provisions for maintaining good health and happiness for a family or persons. It contains sundry items, from sweet jams and jellies, sugary pastries and cookies, with their own distinct attraction to one's own nostrils, that make for not only pleasant inhaling, but also entice the taste buds. There are fruits and vegetables for cooking or eating raw. It is, most appropriately, used for the storing of coffees and teas, all of various flavors and aromas.

Shelves are lined with canned goods, condiments and spices for the enhancing of flavor and the increasing healthiness of the food being served. A multitude of ingredients for baking cakes, pies and various foods for good health and happiness.

Besides precious and delicious food items, a pantry can be used to house bowls for preparing food, pots and pans for the preparation of food, china, teapots, one's teacups and saucers, serving accoutrements, kettles, tablecloths and napkins for different occasions.

A well-stocked pantry, depending upon its proper arrangement and color placement, can be quite beautiful and a delight to the eye gate, very intriguing to look upon, as well as to take in a multitude of fragrances, thus appealing to the senses of both sight and smell.

I think that in my next home there will be the priority of having my own pantry!

Andrea McDougal

Grandmother's Pantry
A Place of Beauty and Wonder

Before I get too close to bringing this book to an end, I simply could not leave out this memory. There are many stories and memories that simply, because of space and content, could not be in this book, but Grandmother's pantry was a very favorite place that I loved to be. It was lovely to look at, and it could not be left out.

It all began when I was a little girl of five and continued on until this last summer visit at Grandmother's, when I was seventeen. I had to make my visits to Grandmother's pantry a secret, because we were not allowed to go into that pantry unless Grandmother sent us there to get something for her. In the beginning of being introduced to such an intriguing place, I was quite tiny in size and so, upon entering Grandmother's pantry, it seemed to be exceptionally large to me. I could go into it, and there would be shelves for storage from the floor all the way to the ceiling to my left and to my right and a larger area straight in front of me. I could sit on Grandmother's step stool, and there was still plenty of room for me to walk around in this room for keeping what was needed to prepare a meal successfully.

At first, it caught my attention, simply because I had never seen a pantry before, and there were delectable fragrances that would draw me into it. But even if I was just getting a glimpse of what was inside, my eyes were drawn to the beautiful colors and graphics, such as the large tin filled with sugar cookies that had a beautiful picture of Buckingham Palace on it and a photo of Queen Elizabeth. And there were other colorful tins for coffee and teas.

Over to my right was where Grandmother kept her everyday teapots and everyday teacups and saucers, dishes and beautiful serving pieces and lovely linens for dressing her tablecloth when there was company. What kept me there was not just the eye candy, but it was the fragrance that would tempt my nostrils to go in, sit down and inhale the many wonderful and tempting aromas that exuded from sugar cookies, fresh fruits, vegetables and teas—especially Earl Gray, Darjeeling and Cinnamon Spice—and from coffees and also from dark rye and pumpernickel breads. I had, for a long time, kept it a secret. That pantry was my secret place to go to experience the unexperienced until the proverbial door to the proverbial pantry was left ajar.

A menagerie of beauty and aromas!

Oh, how I loved to smell Grandmother's sugar cookies!

I call it the proverbial door and pantry because it was my familiar and customary place of escape. I must admit that I had a dreaded fear of Grandmother finding me in her pantry, and one day it happened.

I immediately had to explain to her what I was doing inside of her well-guarded storage place. With a few tears in my eyes and my lips quivering, I proclaimed in self-defense to her, "Grandmother, it is because I love to smell your sugar cookies! I never took one cookie or anything else. I simply liked looking at and smelling everything!" And that was the conclusion to my dilemma. From then on, she would send me into the pantry on a regular basis to get a multitude of things that she needed for cooking—even when it would have been easier for her to get them herself. She would very nonchalantly, with her lips curled into the slightest smile, send me into the wonderful secret pantry garden to get whatever she needed. I was delighted!

My next home will have a very beautiful pantry that will be a delight to the senses, and I will show it off to my children and grandchildren, mother, sisters, nieces, nephews and friends, and they will learn of sugar cookies from England and delicious-tasting teas, and learn the difference between Earl Gray, Darjeeling and Cinnamon Spice.

One Last Adventure Before Leaving for Home

A Cup of "Cheer-Me-Up Tea"

My time with Grandmother in my seventeenth year would be coming to a close, but we had one more trip to take. I was on a mission that I just knew would be successful. Grandmother had planned that we would take a trip to Gulfport and go shopping for the one thing I had my heart set on, a perfectly white pair of shorts!

When we went shopping, we would take a base bus to get off the base and then take a city bus that would take us from the gate entrance of the base to Gulfport, Mississippi. It was Gulfport that would have exactly what I was looking for. It was where Grandmother would always take us shopping. It was imperative that those

156

shorts had to be white, solid white, no rick rack, no embroidery, no flowers, no frills, simply plain white shorts. I just knew when I got them and would wear them that every one of my friends at school would love them, and I would love them on me.

Well, there were no white shorts to be found anywhere in Gulfport, Mississippi! At one of the stores, the clerk said, "Yes, we have white shorts," and she pulled the shorts out of a drawer. They were white all right, but they had embroidered flowers all over them. They were nice flowers and everything, but they were not what I was wanting—perfectly white shorts.

We checked at several more stores, but no white shorts could be found. This was the South. Not just the South, but the Deep South, and you cannot get much more in the South when you are standing on the beach of the Gulf of Mexico.

It is hot in the Deep South, and white shorts were all the rage, but there were no white shorts to be found anywhere. To say the least, I was disappointed, very, disappointed, to the point of great sadness, and Grandmother saw my disappointment.

It was getting time for us to have to return home on the city bus, but we had time to grab a bite to eat before venturing on our way back to the base and getting home in time to have Grandfather's dinner waiting for him! So, we walked into a quaint little diner.

Well, I thought it was a diner. There were lovely plants and paintings of flowers on the walls by local artists and pretty lace tablecloths on the tables. It really was a charming place to stop and get something to hold us over until we had dinner. Little did I know that I would have my first taste of a blueberry scone and a cup of tea. Grandmother ordered. We shared the scone, and each had a cup of tea, and then we were on our way home.

The disappointment in not finding my perfect white shorts soon dissipated as I focused on the delicious blueberry scone and my cup of "Cheer-Me-Up Tea." Grandmother later told me that it reminded her of a little place she would go to when she lived in England. As I look back on this event, I wonder: had I actually been in my first tearoom unawares?

My Last Day at Grandmother's

A Gift of Love and a Cup of "Reassurance Tea"

This was the last day of my summer vacation with Grandmother. The next day I would have to embark upon the Greyhound Bus once again and go home, for school would be opening soon. The weather would be changing because we were already in the hurricane season.

At the end of our stays at Grandmother's, it seemed that the hot and humid air of summer would soon be coming to an end, and the cooler weather would somehow begin to come in, as the hurricanes would blow across our state or a state close to us.

I would soon be starting my senior year in high school. I was excited because the girls in our class who were thinking of becoming nurses would be taking a trip by bus to New Orleans to visit the hospital and school. I was considering going to nursing school in New Orleans after I graduated. I really wanted to be a doctor, but I thought I would check out the nursing school before making any real decision.

I wanted a perm in my hair. My hair was short, and I wanted to look really cute for school starting. So Grandmother gave me a perm, and while we were waiting on it to set, she called me into her bedroom.

She was lying on her bed. She patted the bed and said, "Come here." I protested, because a rule of the house was that once a bed was made you did *not* get on top of the bed and mess it up. I reminded her of her own rule, but she tapped on the bed again and said it was okay. I got on the bed, leaning on one arm and facing her. She said, "I have something for you," and she handed me a box. There was a lovely bracelet sitting in the box. She told me to put it on, and I did. I loved it! Over the years, I wore it many times and fifty-five years later, I still have that cherished bracelet.

Then, out came the curlers from the perm, and I looked absolutely ridiculous. It makes me laugh even now. I thought I was going to be so glamorous and beautiful for the first day of school, and it was just not going to happen. Before we left for the bus station, we had our breakfast and a cup of "Reassurance Tea."

I remember getting on the bus with my treasure Grandmother had given to me, sitting by the window, and waving good-bye to her. She told me softly, "Remember, you will always look better with longer hair."

A cup of "Reassurance Tea" negates any disappointment!

Grandmother's Gifts

*Cloth napkins, embroidered tablecloths, vintage drinking glasses, a ruby glass
scalloped-edged bowl with six small matching bowls, a large orange carnival glass pear
filled with Hershey's Kisses, a beautiful ribbed glass bowl, a serving platter trimmed
in gold and blue, another of blue and white, a large sterling silver serving tray, a sterling
silver teapot, serving spoons and more.*

would have many more visits with my grandmother over the years, either at her home in New Orleans or in Biloxi, where they would eventually retire. I would no longer be a young girl spending her summers with her grandmother.

Grandmother would live in three other places before returning to Biloxi. My grandfather would be stationed in Tucson, Arizona, and they would also be stationed for a while in Bermuda and then they lived in New Orleans. No matter where they were, Grandmother would always send us a box of goodies, filled with her pastries and little gifts, representing where she was at the time.

I remember that she sent us a package from Tucson, and my sister, Lillian, and I each got a sterling silver bracelet with an Indian-type stone in the center of the bracelet. I still have that bracelet. The stone is gone, but I have her gift. When she was in Bermuda, she sent me a container of pink sand from the beaches of Bermuda.

During many of our visits, when I would get to see Grandmother at her home in Biloxi, she would give me a box filled with beautiful vintage items. There were cloth napkins, napkins trimmed with crochet, embroidered tablecloths, vintage drinking glasses, a ruby glass scalloped-edged bowl with six small matching bowls, a large orange carnival glass pear filled with Hershey Kisses that Mother had given to Grandmother when she was just a teenager. There was a beautiful ribbed glass bowl that I loved and used for years. There was a serving platter trimmed in gold and blue and another platter of blue and white. One platter was a large sterling silver serving tray, and there was a sterling silver teapot and serving spoons. And the list goes on.

The Provenance of an Emerald Glass Inkwell

Provenance
"The place, origin and ownership of something."

There was one item Grandmother presented to me to keep and care for, even though I would see her many times more and receive other gifts from her. It was amongst the other things I just shared with you. It was in the very last box she gave me. This one item, she made clear, she was putting into my possession for safe keeping.

It was a beautiful emerald glass inkwell. The emerald glass was overlaid with sterling silver irises, and the perfectly-rounded lid was also in sterling silver.

When Grandmother handed this item to me, she did it in a very nonchalant manner. She said to me, "This belonged to your fifth-great-grandfather." In this way, she passed this precious item to me without even mentioning the name of who this fifth-great-grandfather was. It took me many years to learn about him. I have now had this beautiful emerald green inkwell for fifty-two years, but it was just five years ago when I found out who this fifth-great-grandfather was. You are about to meet this aristocratic tea drinker in the chapter ahead.

A gift to treasure for a lifetime!

The provenance of a beautiful and very old inkwell was a mystery. To whom did this elegant piece of history belong? Fifty-two years later, it was said that the owner was in a direct line to me, Great-grandmother, Grandmother, Mother, sisters, my children, grandchildren and great-grandchildren. Who was this leader, this great man and even those who came before him and after him? Who were these aristocratic tea drinkers of New Orleans, Baton Rouge and Natchez?

French Tea-Drinking Aristocrats

Tea hit France in the 1600s, long before it would be found in Great Britain. However, it was a very expensive commodity and, therefore, could only be found among the French aristocracy, trusted authorities who ruled under the monarch.

Who Were the Aristocrats?

The aristocrats (also known as nobles) were a select group of people who ruled under the authority of the monarch of various countries. These monarchs included the kings and queens of places like the United Kingdom, parts of Africa, France, Russia, India and others. Only sovereigns had the power to bestow aristocratic titles upon anyone in their realm. These titles included Lords and Ladies, Dukes and Duchesses, Earls and Countesses, Marquesses and Marchionesses, Viscounts and Viscountesses, Barons and Baronesses. Such a ranking left a person only lower than the monarch, and the title could only be given for being landowners, great military leaders, other great leaders and the intelligent and wealthy.

Who Were These Aristocratic Tea Drinkers Of New Orleans, Baton Rouge and Natchez?

A Cup of "Legacy Tea"

I find it delightful and heartwarming that such great leaders have been found to be my ancestors, great-grandfathers, great-uncles, etcetera. They were some of the early prominent citizens of New Orleans. One of them, in particular, helped to found and form my own city, Baton Rouge, Louisiana, where I have lived now for almost 50 years and also the city of Natchez (named for the Natchez Indians) in what is now Mississippi. His name, in French, was Charles Louis Montbrun Boucher De Grand Pre.

Grand Pre was born October 25, 1745 in New Orleans and was christened at the Saint Louis Cathedral in that city. His father, Louis Antoine De Grand Pre, along with other French families, was part of the second expulsion of French Acadians by the British from Nova Scotia. This was a voluntary expulsion, unlike the first forced expulsion.

Louis Antoine married a New Orleans girl. Their son, Don Carlos De Grand Pre (as the Spanish called him), was my fifth-great-grandfather, and he was the owner of the beautiful emerald green inkwell that once belonged to and was gifted and handed down to me by my grandmother.

How could it be that all the pieces of this very large puzzle could just happen to fall into my lap? It was through a very persistent and dear friend, Rachel Shaw, who happened to be a part of my ministry since 1996. She is an active member of the DAR, the Daughters of the American Revolution, and was very persistent in asking my permission to do my genealogy. I was hesitant at first but finally gave in to her pleas. I was very sure that she would only find the simplest of people and nothing out of the ordinary. Then, shortly thereafter, I received a phone call from her, and she began to unfold the mystery of my family line. Soon I felt credence to the mysterious emerald green inkwell. We soon were able to meet together, and she began to show me the most fascinating writings about my family, and we sat down and had a cup of "Legacy Tea."

Afternoon tea was the common practice of my fifth-great-grandfather, Charles Louis Montbrun Boucher de Grand Pre and his family and sometimes an indulgence in a thick, hot chocolate!

Grand Pre was a title given to my fifth-great-grandfather and his father by the King of France. It meant "Lord of Grand Pre," Grand Pre being a place in Nova Scotia. There were Lords, Dukes, Earls, Marquesses, Viscounts and Barons. These titles were bestowed upon them. They were the aristocrats or nobles of their society, ranked only lower than the monarch. Such an aristocratic title could only come from a king or a queen. The title was given for being landowners, great military leaders, those possessing great capacity for leadership and intelligence.

Grand Pre, a Frenchman, would serve under Spanish rule here in Louisiana as a Commandant over many of the parishes. He would then become one of the first governors of Louisiana under Spanish rule. He built the first governor's mansion in Mississippi. It was called Grand Pre.

During this time, Louisiana was known as West Feliciana or West Florida. Only after the Louisiana Purchase from France did the name change to Louisiana, when the state was no longer under Spanish rule.

In 1805, Grand Pre was hired by Spain to establish the first community in Baton Rouge. He called it Spanish Town, and it lies in the heart of modern-day Baton Rouge next to the New State Capitol building. Spanish Town was established because the Spanish families of the Canary Islands did not wish to live on French soil. To this day, Spanish Town is still a quaint and beautiful historic district that is very desirable to live in, and it still bears the original name Grand Pre gave it so long ago.

In 1806, there would be another community that would be formed, not far from Spanish Town. It has also become a Historic District in downtown Baton Rouge. Grand Pre would be asked to help with the laying out of the streets to this new community. It was laid out in the European style of an X and was known as Beauregard Town. The founding father of Beauregard Town was Elias Beauregard, and the Beauregards are also among our noble ancestors, having married the daughter of one of those French Cavaliers of New Orleans. (I will get to the Caveliers soon).

Beauregard Town Historic District, just like Spanish Town, still bears its original name, and one of main streets in the X is named Grand Pre. It also remains to this day a very sought-after area of Baton Rouge to live in because of its charming architecture and beautiful gardens.

Two Cavalier brothers arrived in New Orleans before 1770 from Normandy, France. They were cousins of the famous René-Robert Cavelier, Sieur de La Salle, or simply La Salle, as most school children know him. It is said that he also took several of his Cavelier cousins with him on his explorations. La Salle explored the Mississippi and discovered its mouth in 1682. Years later, his cousins would follow in his footsteps to Louisiana

Charlotte Sophie de Grand Pre, the second daughter of Charles Louis was born in Natchez in 1789 and married my fourth-great-grandfather, Antoine Joseph Cavelier in 1809. He was born in New Orleans in 1773, the first generation of Caveliers born in the New World.

Rene Robert Cavelier Sieur de La Salle

Rene Robert Cavelier, our ancestor, was a French explorer given the title Sieur de La Salle by the King of France, King Louis XIV, for La Salle committing to find land in the New World for France. In 1682 the explorer claimed the entire Mississippi basin for France and named it La Louisiana after King Louis.

The Court of Two Sisters Restaurant in New Orleans

Leading up to 1726, the address that would eventually house the Court of Two Sister Restaurant, would not be known as Royal Street, but would be called Governors Row. It was home to five governors, two state supreme court justices and one future justice of the U. S. Supreme Court. Zachary Taylor, who later became the 12th President of the United States, also resided there.

In 1832, there was a great economic boom in New Orleans, and the original property was purchased by my ancestor, my great-uncle, Jean Baptiste Zenon Cavelier (he was President of the Bank of New Orleans), and there he built the current beautiful structure which is known today as the Court of Two Sisters Restaurant.

Jean Baptiste and his brother, my fourth-great-grandfather, Antoine Joseph Cavelier (who married Grand Pre's daughter, Charlotte Sophie), both operated antique stores, the one at 613 Royal Street (the current street name) and two doors down at 631 Royal Street. They were purveyors of fine art, antiques, beautiful French teapots, teacups, the finest of china and fine wines.

Those of you who have been to the Court of Two Sisters fully know of the beautiful courtyard for dining. Well, my great-uncle, his lovely wife, Marie Louise, and their five children lived on the second and third floors of the place they called home, and the courtyard was used to host beautiful and exquisite balls.

Patti's Court in New Orleans

Adelani Patti, the most famous Italian soprano opera singer in history, would visit the homes and businesses of the Caveliers of New Orleans.

My great-uncle, Jean Baptiste Zenon Cavelier, the builder of the current building known worldwide as the Court of Two Sisters Restaurant and the President of the Bank of New Orleans, and my fourth-great-grandfather Antoine Joseph Cavalier, commonly called "Jeune" or "Petit," as I mentioned previously, were purveyors of fine art, French antiques, teapots, teacups and beautiful china. The present-day address of their previously-owned properties is 631-635 Royal Street in the beautiful French Quarter of New Orleans. Their two-story building became known as "Patti's Court" due to the fact that the world-renowned Italian soprano opera singer would often visit these two Cavalier families and perform in the courtyard. They eventually gave her the property to be used as an opera house.

Teatime at Patti's Court was always an enchanting time filled with the clanging of beautiful china, exquisite teapots and guests who would come from all over the world.

Mother

and a Cup of "New Orleans Tea"

At many different times, as Mother was growing up in New Orleans, she and Terry and their mother, my grandmother Laurel, lived in the heart of the French Quarter. When Mother was a young teenager, Grandmother was operating an antique store that belonged to Ma Mère and Ma Père (Richard and Sarah Cavelier), and they lived in a small house behind a large old building on Royal Street.

Every weekday morning, when they got up, Grandmother would take Terry and walk across the street to operate the Cavalier antique shop, and Mother would set out on foot through the French Quarter to school. At every business she passed there would be men, young and old, washing down the sidewalks and the streets, preparing for the day's business. These men would tell her, "Good morning, Lil Miss. Don't you be afraid now. We are watching for you, going to school and coming home, cause we are going to protect you, and we won't let anyone hurt you." As she went along to McDonough High School and back home, they greeted her, both young and old, as Lil Miss.

After her day at school, Mother again made her way on foot back through the French Quarter, then went to help Grandmother at the Cavalier antique store. There, in the shop, the two of them would have an afternoon cup of "New Orleans Tea." Every night, they went to sleep to the sounds of jazz that wafted up and down the streets of the French Quarter.

Memories are golden threads woven through our hearts and minds that no one can remove.

Andrea McDougal

Jazz derives from the slang word "jasm," which originally meant energy, vitality, spirit and pep. It has been called America's only original art form.

In Closing

We have now come to the closing of my first tea book, A Southern Lady's Tea Journey. It is truly only a small portion of the beautiful memories associated with my childhood, and there is oh, so much more to my life's journey that has brought me to this point and the habit of having tea. I recently read that when you write a book of the memories of your life, you get to relive that life. How very true this is! In writing this book, I chose to focus on that which was good and "of a good report." Therefore, the reliving of my childhood through this book has brought me great joy and happiness! I hope you have enjoyed reading and that you will be looking for the next Tea Garden Publication, A Southern Lady's Tea Adventures. This book will have an international flare to it. It will have stories of all the different countries and the unusual places and people I have had tea with. There will be delicious recipes that you can use at your own personal teas from countries like Australia, the Philippines and the U. S.—delicious, easy and beautiful recipes from well-seasoned cooks who are "lovers of everything tea" and "lovers of everything beautiful."

The next book, A Southern Lady's Teas, will be about the different teas I have done and helped to do, including a Presidential Inaugural Tea and a Governor's Inaugural Tea. I thought that I would whet your appetite just a little bit.

Andrea "Andy" McDougal
Tea Garden Publications

Hold fast to your dreams,
for without them life is
a broken-winged bird that cannot fly.

—Langston Hughes—

You can never get a cup of tea large enough or a book
long enough to suit me.

—C. S. Lewis—

The Adventure begins with Tea.

Spanish Town

East of this point
was Spanish Town, laid out
in 1805 by
Carlos de GrandPre,
Governor of Spanish
West Florida for the
Canary Islanders from
Galvez Town that they
might continue to live
on Spanish soil and help
to defend the fort.
Spanish Town Road

SPANISH TOWN

1805

Spanish Town

Founded by 5th-Great-Grandfather Don Carlos Luis Boucher De Grand Pre

Governor of Louisiana under Spanish rule.

*Grand Pre
assisted with
the layout of
Beauregard
Town*

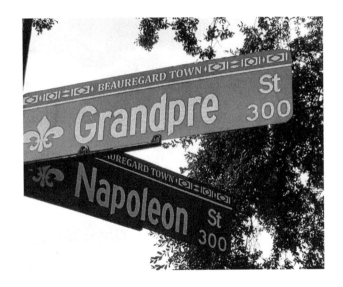

European layout in an **X**

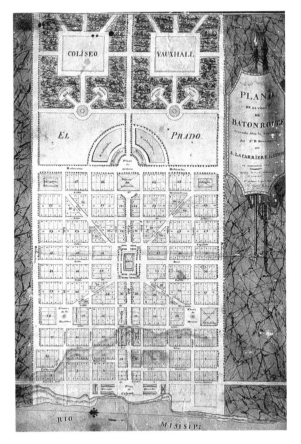

Court of Two Sisters

Built by Great-Uncle Jean Baptiste Zenon Cavelier

Beautiful courtyard day and night

Author Contact

I welcome your comments and suggestions.

Tea.Garden.Publications@gmail.com
Phone: 225-572-9844
www.facebook.com/andrea.mcdougal.3
www.facebook.com/andymcdougalministries
www.instagram/andrea.mcdougal.3
www.instagram/asouthernladysteas

Other Books
by Andrea "Andy" McDougal

The Glory of God Revealed

His Wonders in the Deep

Your Camels Are Coming

Understanding the Seed

The Arrows of the Lord

The Power of the Seed

Latest Edition

CPSIA information can be obtained
at www.ICGtesting.com
Printed in the USA
LVHW072020041121
702388LV00001B/9